A Queen's Ransom

The Story of Esther

by Nansii Downer

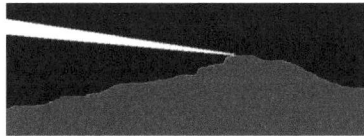

Light Point Press

A Queen's Ransom: The Story of Esther

© 2012 Nansii Downer

Published by Light Point Press
www.LightPointPress.com

All scripture quotation from the New King James Version, © Copyright Thomas Nelson, Inc., 1990, 1985, 1983. Used by permission.

Printed in the United States of America

ISBN: 13: 978-0615742342

Other books by Nansii Downer

'The Redemption of Ruth'
'Better Late Than Never'

www.NansiiDowner.com

Dedication

The story of Esther is filled with adventure, espionage, thrills and chills. It is a classic battle of good versus evil. When you think about it, any well-known mystery writer would love to put their name as the author of this timeless work. The twists and turns, the ins and outs, the intricate weaving of a story within a story...well for an author it just doesn't get any better than this.

Good guys, really bad guys and a young heroine named Esther, who hears the words from her uncle "For such a time as this" and steps into a world of elegance, majesty and a the mighty Persian king whose heart she wins.

This book is dedicated to the Esther in all of us. The still small voice that we hear telling us to do this and to trust in that. Esther heard it and she quietly, yet firmly rose to the occasion. She risked her life to save the lives of her people. Most of us will never be asked to do that. But, if we were, could we do as she did? For the love of Christ and from the love of Christ we most likely could.

Special Thanks

To our son, Jaymes for an excellent cover photo and to our beloved daughter in law, Jordan, who modeled for the cover and shares the character of Esther.

Introduction

It's been a relatively quiet time in Jewish history, at least to the untrained eye that is. But deep in the heart of three unforgettable men burns a personal rage so strong that it can make or break who they are now and who they are meant to be.

Ahasuerus, the mighty King of Persia.
Haman, the crafty "kings right hand man."
Mordecai, a quiet respectable Jewish businessman living within the citadel of Sushan.

Each carries a burden of anger and grief. Each has the problems of a nation on their shoulders. Each try to do the impossible until each meets their match in Esther.

This is no fairy tale story or is it? A rags to riches, come up from the ditches story that will leave you breathless and waiting for the "happy ending." There are many fairy tale stories but throughout the ages there has only been one...

...ESTHER

Chapter 1

Come with me as we travel to a bustling city in the Persian Empire. *Shushan* is the Hebrew word for the citadel here, and in Greek the word is *Susa*. This is one of the four capital cities of this vast empire. The others were: Babylon, Ecbatana and Persopolis. Shushan was used as the winter residence for King Ahasuerus, as well as the other Persian kings.

The citadel, which is another word for a city, would have been heavily fortified and equipped to protect the royal family while they were staying there. In looking further at the word "citadel," it actually means more than just "city." Webster's Dictionary says it is a "fortress that commands a city." That speaks more of the buildings and the palace, which makes perfect sense. Just as the daily business in the book of Ruth was done at the city gates, the business of the empire would have been handled at the citadel.

Since the royal palace was located there, it is easy to imagine how vast the area must have been. In reading about this kingdom, I found that some historians and archeologists have recorded the citadel to be six to seven miles in circumference. In 1852 a British archeologist by the name of W.K. Loftus identified the site in Shushan when he discovered an inscription of Artaxerxes II that reads: "My ancestor Darius built this palace in former times. In the reign of my grandfather (Artaxerxes I), it was burned. I have restored it." Archaeologists have been excavating the site for the last 100 years. Many of the artifacts from these ancient cities and kingdoms are in museums around the world. Isn't that amazing? Even today, we are still learning about the people and places of Biblical times.

The palace at Shushan was opulent and impressive to say the least. Its splendor and ornate designs and furnishing spoke of a kingdom of great wealth and even greater excess. As we study this book we will see that King Ahasuerus, the king of the Persian Empire at the time of Esther, is a great example of the effects of excessive wealth and power.

There are only two books in the Bible that have a woman's name for a title, Esther and Ruth. Each of these small books carries a wealth of information about God and His people. There is ONE very important difference though between these books. Do you know what it is? Let's see if we can discover it together, OK?

Chapter 2

Have you ever read the Bible in chronological order? There are versions of the Bible that are written this way to help us understand the timelines and how the different books connect to each other. While studying the Book of Esther my readings traveled back and forth in the books of 1st and 2nd Kings, 1st and 2nd Chronicles, Ezra and Daniel. The timeline for the occurrences in Esther put it right between chapters 6 and 7 of Ezra, which was about 483-473 BC.

The Achaemenid Dynasty that controlled the vast Persian Empire was the ruling family and was led by Cyrus the Great. The land mass is substantial and would be approximately the size of the United States of America. It included Asia, Africa and parts of Europe. It stretched from modern day Spain to modern day India. The Persian Empire was the most powerful and influential empire in the ancient world ruling from approximately 550-330 BC when the Greeks conquered them. There are many books and commentaries written about this period of time. I could go into greater detail about this time period, but maybe we should save it for another day.

As we begin reading chapter 1:1, the king is in Shushan. The Greek name for this king is Xerxes 1 and the Hebrew rendition is Ahasuerus (a-HAS-you--AIR-us), which is the transliteration of the Persian name, Khshayarsha. The word Ahasuerus is not actually his name but a title meaning "venerable king" or even "high father", much like the words Caesar or President which are used to identify the position of the person. Since we learned in our previous study of the book of Ruth that Shushan was a winter residence for the royal family, then we can assume it is wintertime or the end of the winter season. Our past study in Ruth revealed that the rulers usually set out on their conquests in the springtime, so the winter months could very possibly be a time of strategizing and planning.

As you will see from verse 3, the king has invited his officials and important leaders from the many provinces of the kingdom to a great feast. A great feast indeed, I would say, since it lasted about six months!!! Can you imagine having to entertain company at your house for six months??? A few days is about all I can take. But here we read that the king has invited the "officials and servants -the powers of Persia and Media, the nobles and the princes" to come to the palace and enjoy a grand feast. Obviously the king had something important he wanted to discuss with them. I find it hard to believe that he just wanted to show them a good time at the palace. He was planning something, and he needed their allegiance in order to carry it out.

Once again we must look back in history to get an idea what the king was planning and why. This king was the son of Darius I. His mother was the daughter of Cyrus the Great, the founder of the Persian Empire. Royal blood and allegiance to the empire flowed in his veins. Darius I had invaded Greece back in 490 and been trounced for his efforts and defeated at the Battle of Marathon. In 486 BC, as Darius was preparing to return to Greece for another takeover attempt, he died. Once his loyal son, Ahasuerus was on the throne, he felt compelled to return to Greece and conquer it in an effort to avenge his father and to expand the empire.

This was the reason for the invitation to the great feast. He needed complete support and loyalty from his subjects. He needed to impress them with his massive wealth to prove that the empire could afford to take on this battle for dominance in Greece. According to the Greek historian Herodotus, the King's desire was to completely take over Greece by taking over Europe. His desire was to bring the entire world's population and land under one kingdom. The Persian Kingdom. It seems to me that I remember another military leader who felt the same way about his "kingdom" in World War II. Does anyone know who I am referring to?

So, the stage has now been set. The king has invited his military leaders and community leaders to come and spend time with him at Shushan. This is a huge gathering of people lasting six months. Can you even comprehend the cost of such an affair? Millions and millions of dollars I am sure. I can't fathom the amount of time, energy and preparation that would be involved. The preparation for the food would have been a 24/7 duty. The butcher, the baker and the candlestick maker were busy, busy, BUSY!!

But the party is not over. Nope. If you look at verse 5, another party follows this one! My, my, my, this king does love to party, doesn't he? Let's meet back here tomorrow and take a look at the next party in the king's busy schedule.

Chapter 3

Do any of you remember the song "Garden Party" by Ricky Nelson? I have probably dated myself here, but it came to my mind as I was studying this part of the scripture passage for today. The first four verses of Esther tell us about the king, the citadel and the great banquet he hosts for the leaders of the Persian Empire. Now the six month feast has ended and the king hosts another banquet that lasts another seven days. But the guests here are quite a bit different. He includes everyone from the "least to the greatest" to come to the royal gardens and eat, drink and by all means, be merry.

I enjoy watching television shows about travel, the ones that take you places you would probably never get to see. Castles in Scotland. The marketplace in India. A jostling ride in the back of a jeep on an African Safari. The Royal Gardens in England. I can just sit and watch and let my imagination take over and see myself walking through the gardens, smelling the fragrant multicolored flowers or sitting peacefully by a small waterfall and hearing the peaceful sound of the water on the stones. Now, take that picture and multiply it by about a hundred, and you just might begin to see what the royal gardens at Shushan might have been like.

In this section of the chapter, the writer is very careful and precise as he (or she) describes the banquet in the garden. No mention in verses 1-4 about the sheer beauty and opulence of the banquet hall. I wonder why? Some theologians believe that the author of the book of Esther may have been Mordecai, Ezra or Nehemiah because whoever wrote it had a great knowledge of the palace and paid close attention to detail. I won't speculate as to who might have written the book. I am really grateful though that they did, aren't you? These few verses paint a beautiful picture of the splendor and grandeur of these gardens.

I have read that the palace itself was about two and a half acres in size. That works out to be about 109,000 square feet – big house! Can you just imagine the size of the gardens that surrounded it? Verse 6 describes the linens hanging from the marble pillars. But what caught my eye was the flooring. "Mosaic pavement of porphyry, marble, mother-of-pearl and other costly stones" were used. These gardens were outside and look at the amount of finery with which they were decorated!! Couches of gold and silver???? Individually made and uniquely different golden wine goblets? And to think, all these years I have been trying to keep a matched set of glasses for our company to use!

The "things" and possessions of this kingdom were over the top by anyone's standards. And that was exactly the point. King Ahasuerus needed his loyal subjects, servants and leaders to see how rich he was and how great the empire was. He needed to "sell" them on his plan, and the best way to do that was to prove it was worth it to them and to the empire they served.

And so, the mighty King Ahasuerus shows off all that is in his palace and gardens. But wait. Is there more yet to come of his showing off? Will he stop here in the garden of plenty, or does he have more that he wants to parade in front of his visitors?

Chapter 4

As we near the end of the festive banquet out in the gardens of the citadel, let's take a closer look at Esther 1:7-8 for just a moment. Remember when we read that each of the golden drinking vessels were different and unique? That in itself is a great feat since we are talking about hundreds of guests coming to these parties, many, even thousands, over the six plus months. The idea hit me that the uniqueness and "oneness" of these vessels had more meaning to this king than I originally thought.

Most people that I know would absolutely be astounded if the fine china, silverware and goblets didn't match. We consider the exact replica and matching to be the artistry or craftsmanship. But here, the writer makes certain that he lets us know of the uniqueness and individuality of the golden goblets. Why? I think once again, that this unusual creation of one-of-a-kind goblets spoke of not only the magnitude of wealth that the Persian Kingdom possessed, but it spoke of a powerful and controlling king that was able to order and receive this most unusual request. It showed the power that he had over even the artisans of his kingdom. It is the smallest of details to perfection and the noticeability of the craft that caught my eye here. He paid attention to the detail of the goblets, and he achieved his goal. Power - artfully displayed in wine goblets. Subtle, yet convincing.

The next portion of the verse really and truly speaks of his total control. He *let* each man drink as much or as little as he wanted. You see, Ahasuerus had the control to decide and enforce how much each person drank. My, my, my! Verse 8 says that "according to the law, the drinking was not compulsory." Remember how the ice skaters at the

Olympics all perform their compulsory routines? That means that they each must do the exact same skating moves that the judges of the competition require. It was the same here in this kingdom. At some point in time there had been, and possibly still was, a decree that the king could order you to drink whatever amount that he saw fit for you to drink. Very dangerous and very controlling. People do lots of "not so smart" things when they have had too much to drink. This would be a recipe for disaster for the participants.

Dr. J. Vernon McGee, in his commentary on this book, calls the events of the banquets "pagan from beginning to end." At first, I didn't understand that comment at all. I saw no idol worship within the first few verses, at least no *blatant* idol worship. It is not like King Ahasuerus had a golden cow as the centerpiece for all to see. No, the pagan act of idol worship was all done obscurely. I probably wouldn't have even noticed had I not read Dr. McGee's commentary either. But I did, and now I see it. The idol of worship was the party giver himself. The mighty King of Persia.

Each of us has opportunity from time to time to go and visit friends. Friends whose homes we may never have been in or at least visited for a very long time. Or maybe our friends bought a new home and we are going to pay a housewarming call. We go there and silently look around and take it all in. The furniture. The photographs. The fancy bedding with the abundance of matching pillows. The guest bathroom with the cutest little embroidered hand towels. The kitchen with all new and very expensive granite countertops. Is anyone following my train of thought here? Inside of us, we kind of look around and secretly groan to have what they have. Or, we ask ourselves why we have so little in comparison to them. And then it happens. Lust and idol worship.

Things we don't really need become the very things that we feel we must have. We deserve them. They are owed to us. We want to have what the "Joneses" have. We almost burn inside with the lust of desire for "things." From sea to shining sea or from any coast to coast in the world it happens every day, a lust after things of the world. This is the idol worship that I speak of for King Ahasuerus. What he had wasn't enough. He wanted more and more. Land, servants, THINGS!!! Why? Because he was the most important person in his life. He was his own idol.

It seems that the king had many months now to show off all of his kingdom, his array of delicious food, the plentiful and flowing wine that caused him to be "merry." There couldn't possibly be anything left in the kingdom that his guests haven't seen. Or was there? Was there *one* more prized possession that the king just must show off to his guests? We will see.

Chapter 5

Today we start in the 9th verse of chapter one. Here we see that Queen Vashti has also hosted a party for the ladies of the kingdom. And it is within this section that I have come to the conclusion that alas, I must report, that there is absolutely no way that a woman penned the words of this book. Oh, I know, it doesn't really say that it is not written by a woman, but if you read between the lines, I am sure that you (at least my female friends) will agree with me. Why do I feel so strongly about it? Well, it's easy really. There is no mention of the clothing, the shoes, the makeup or even a hint about any hairstyles worn by these women!! Trust me here, I know too many women who could not have attended such an affair and not made mention of the attire. Don't you?

Here is another thing that I noticed. The scripture is not specific in the amount of time that the Queen hosted the gathering either. In the previous verses, particular attention is given to making certain that the reader knows how long the party lasted. But here, no mention of a timeline. I wonder why. Could it be that the "women's gathering" was of no real importance to the king? Remember, he was out to impress the men of the kingdom. I also took note that the women were not present in the garden area with the men either. It would have been a social "faux pas" for the women to join the men. This made me think about old television shows where the men "would retire to the library for a brandy and a cigar." The women always retired to the sitting room or parlor by themselves and worked on their tapestries, needlework and such. Have I dated myself yet again?

Verse 10 starts off by letting us know that on the seventh day, the king's heart was merry with wine. I would venture to say that this king's heart was "merry with wine" on most of the days of these banquets, wouldn't you? In my readings about him, I have found him to be a man intent on bringing pleasure to himself. The king did what the king desired to do and didn't really give much thought to how others would feel or react. Some call him impetuous. As I said before, I call him arrogant and selfish.

Right in the middle of this soiree, he calls for seven of his eunuchs to go and fetch Queen Vashti and oh yes, make sure she is wearing her "royal crown." Did you know that in ancient Persia the royal kings were sometimes so enamored with themselves and their great wealth that they would even have precious jewels and gemstones attached to their beards???? Now, if they would put these jewels and gems in their beard (and please think of all of the men you know that get food stuck in their beards) how much fancier and ornate the royal crowns must have been!

Ah, but here, the royal crown was not just to be worn and shown off for the visitors to see and be jealous over. No. It was the *"wearer"* of the crown that the king wanted his court to pay attention to, Queen Vashti. She was to be the crowning glory of his party. He was going to have her parade around in front of all of the "tipsy" men in the garden. I have read that he may have wanted her to dance for them, which, as his wife, would have been totally out of line. She was the Queen of Persia, not some harlot or some palace prostitute. But, for whatever reason, he sends his eunuchs to go and bring her to him. Not a request. Not a suggestion. It was a command. From the king.

I cannot for one moment think how the faces of the eunuchs must have had looked when she said "No!" Can you just picture seven little eunuchs looking from one to another and then drawing straws to see which of them would have to relay the message to the king? They would have been shaking in their sandals folks. No one, absolutely NO ONE tells the king "No." Nope, not ever.

Some commentaries differ on the reason why Queen Vashti stood her ground and refused to be subjected to a drunken, rowdy group of men. I have even read that she may have been pregnant with their son at the time. Whatever her reasoning, she refused to participate. Some say, and I must agree, that her refusal may have made the king look weak in the eyes of his guests. But there is a part of me that says Vashti had confidence in herself and in her marriage. She may have felt that if he were not "merry with wine," he would not have asked her to do this. Maybe her hope was that when the party was over she could explain to him why she refused. Maybe, just maybe, she hoped that good old fashioned common sense would prevail and in the morning, the king, her husband, would be apologetic for even suggesting such a thing in the first place. Maybe?

Let's see how this plays out.

Chapter 6

I would like to spend a bit of time getting to know Queen Vashti. In verses 9-12, in the middle of her banquet for the ladies of the kingdom, the king summons her to come to his banquet and be put on display for all of his "merry of heart" male friends. But let's focus on the queen and see what we can learn about her.

The Queen of Persia, Vashti, is the daughter of King Belshazzar, the last king of Babylon. She is the great-granddaughter of King Nebuchadnezzar. Does anyone remember who he is and his relationship to the Jewish nation? Go and get a fresh cup of coffee and open your Bible to 2 Kings 25 and the verses will help you to remember who this king was.

Vashti, whose name is derived from Persian words meaning "beautiful woman" is surprised by an attack from the Medes and Persians on her father's palace. She has no idea that her father has been killed and goes to his room to find him and seek protection. Instead of the safety of her father's arms, she finds Darius I in her father's sleeping quarters. Instead of killing her on the spot, Darius, maybe in a show of pity towards this young woman, captures her and takes her back to Persia. But he doesn't save her because it was the right thing to do. No. He brings her back as a gift to his son!!! She will be married to his son AND become the Queen of Persia. Does anybody want to take a guess at who this Persian "son" might be? That's right. It is none other than Ahasuerus.

Just as Ahasuerus was using his wealth and influence on his kingdom, his father had done the same thing by the arranged marriage of Vashti to Ahasuerus. Politics, folks. Pure and simple. Look around you. Even in our cutting edge society of today, the same type of politics are played out each day. The relationship of this king and queen played an important role in the growth of the Persian nation. Why? I am not sure, since I have wondered and pondered how Vashti could have ever had anything to do with the family that killed her father. It escapes me as to how or why Darius would have put her in the position of becoming queen in the first place. Wouldn't her loyalty be elsewhere?

Perhaps Vashti feared for her very life. Maybe Darius was even using her as a trophy.

If there is one thing that I have learned about King Ahasuerus these last few weeks it is that he "wants what he wants when he wants it," and nothing or no one is to stand in his way. In verse 12 we read that when Vashti refused the king's command, "he was furious and that his anger burned within him." Have you ever gotten that angry at someone? Where you are just seething inside? You have a million words that you want to spew at them. Your heart is pounding in your chest because your blood pressure has gone sky high. Has this ever happened to you???? I know it has to me. And I must confess, it has not been a pretty sight either!!

Will the mighty king take a moment and "count to 10?" Will he turn from his anger and cool down before confronting the situation? Or will he go head first, fists clenched and teeth barred in a fit of rage as he deals with the situation?

Chapter 7

As we continue our study we are looking at Esther 1:13-20. The party in the garden has come to an abrupt stop. The king has received the news from one of his eunuchs, that Queen Vashti will not be joining in the festivities.. Can you just almost hear him bellow, "WHAT?????"

Notice in verse 15, the king says "What shall *we* do to Queen Vashti?" He is speaking here to his close legal advisors, the ones in his kingdom who know Persian law much better than he does. After all, a king doesn't need to *know* everything; he just needs to have folks in his court who do. There are seven princes of Medea and Persia close by to offer him words of advice. Please take note that this is the same number of eunuchs that the king sent to go and get Vashti. It made me wonder if the Persian culture had a thing for the number seven. Oh, wait... isn't it the Bible that calls the number seven the number of perfection? Somehow I seriously doubt that King Ahasuerus cared about the Word of God. No, in all reality, these seven princes were representatives of the seven lands that he had conquered.

As in any circumstance or time when decisions need to be made, it is always a good idea to seek wise counsel. Perhaps, Ahasuerus and his wife should seek some wise counsel right about now. What do you think? The Bible is full of instances where the greatest lesson learned could very simply be the one about "seeking wise counsel". It would almost be impossible to start at Genesis and work forward and not be able to notice the many, many times when "talking it out" and seeking someone else's input very well might have changed the outcome. How many times have you looked back on an unpleasant situation that you were involved in with the afterthought "why didn't I just ASK?" Sometimes it almost haunts you? You respond a certain way, or say something that you wish a hundred times you could take back. Wise counsel helps us to stop, look and listen. Like the wise counsel we learned years ago about crossing the street. We still teach it to our own kids today.

Vashti, in her refusal to come to the gardens, has displayed three very severe and punishable offenses. She has denied the authority of a man, she has denied the authority of her husband and she has denied the authority of the king. Don't brush over this, ya'll. These were indeed very serious offenses for any woman of that day. Our Bible study friend Marilyn wrote and asked me if it could have been that Vashti did indeed harbor ill feelings for the Persian kingdom, and this was the reason for her denying the king. Somehow, I felt the same way. As I asked, how could she possibly have even been civil to the family that killed her father and her people? Remember, she was a Babylonian princess before she was captured and given to Ahasuerus.

Human emotions are the foundational cement of our human "building". Our bodies and souls are nourished and replenished by the feeling we get from loving and of being loved. The Lord, in His mighty wisdom, designed us this way. We are *supposed* to feel, we are *supposed* to laugh and cry and sing and dance.

From the joyful uplifting voices raised in songs of praise to our King to the wail of the broken hearted searching for solace from that same King, the range of human emotion runs wide. Without our emotions, we would have no idea how to praise or why we cry. But taming our emotions, keeping them under control, is something that each of us struggle with daily.

Countless times I have embarrassed myself by being so mad, angry, or so hurt by a situation, that I broke down in tears right in front of the person who was the cause of this distress. I was beyond consoling. I was way past thinking clearly. All I wanted was for them to admit that I was RIGHT!!! Hurtful words, cutting remarks, glaring stares. Oh, it makes my skin crawl with remorse for all the times that my emotions got the best of me. I wish that I could go back and "stop, look and listen" for safe crossing. That is where wise counsel comes in.

As King Ahasuerus leans back on his throne, burning with anger towards Vashti, will those around him help him to stop, look and listen or will they jump right into this moment of "mad"-ness and lend their two cents to an already bad situation? While there is wisdom in using the counsel of others (Prov. 11:14), we must remember to seek the counsel of the Lord, which stands forever (Ps. 33:11). Let's see what "All the King's Men" have to say.

Chapter 8

So here we are, looking over the shoulder of the mighty King Ahasuerus and his princely princes as they try to decide what to do with good Queen Vashti. Before we get into that though, I would like to share something with you about the wiles and ways of alcohol.

One of the most devastatingly cunning tools in Satan's arsenal is the mighty glass of intoxicating drink. It has brought good men and women to their knees and left families crippled for years struggling to repair the damage. If you think that the abuse of alcohol is NOT a tool of Satan, think again my friend, think again. For the most part and for most people, there is nothing wrong with an occasional drink. I have nothing against that. It is what happens when it is abused and used in excess that I want to share with you.

I was raised in the 60's. It was a time when men would return home from work in the evening and many celebrated with the "cocktail hour." I remember the kitchen cabinet in our home in Anaheim, California being stocked to capacity with any kind of alcohol that could possibly be mixed into a Highball, Martini, Bloody Mary or Screw Driver. My parents and their friends would gather together and laugh and talk and drink and laugh and talk and drink some more. It was like a nightly ritual in our neighborhood. And the weekends????? Well, that was a blur of more laughing, talking and a whole bunch of drinking. Except this. At some point in all of the festivities, the laughing and talking got to be less and the drinking got to be more. A whole bunch more.

My stepfather (who I was raised with) was a huge man. And when he drank, let me tell you, he got even bigger!! My mother (who passed away when I was almost 20) got louder and angrier. I am not sure why either because as a child it seemed like they were just happy and I had no idea why each of them changed. But change they did. And not for the better either.

As time went on the punishments that came to me when the drinking occurred is something that I will always remember. You see, my stepdad blamed me because my mother was drunk by the time he got home from work. My mother would be passed out on the couch without any dinner in the oven, and that made for a really crummy evening for him. So his rage was taken out on me. He was in control. He could do with me as he pleased, and there was nothing in this world that I could do to stop him. The beatings were hard and fast. My mother blamed her unhappiness and drinking on me so the beatings I got were my punishment for making her an alcoholic.

My mother had been diagnosed with cervical cancer, and in her mind I had somehow given it to her when she was pregnant with me. She carried the fear of dying and her anger so deep within her that her blaming me for it came as easily as breathing. And since she chose to drink her way to oblivion each day, then it was even easier for my stepdad to blame me for her drunkenness, therefore his anger at me and his punishments were then justified in his mind. Do you see the tools of Satan at work here?

Growing up in that kind of environment left me with an emptiness and a longing that I could never quite quench. I so very much wanted to be loved and accepted. I so very much wanted to feel someone's hands on me in a loving way, not the hands that would slap me backwards up a flight of stairs. I searched for years to find someone, anyone, that could forgive me for these terrible sins that I had somehow committed. I vowed I would never touch alcohol and that I would be different than my mother was. Easier said than done, I am afraid.

As much as I knew firsthand about how alcohol could ruin a family, I still chose to reach for it when my life became so miserable. Satan knew full well what ploy of relaxation and escape to place in front of me. "A little glass of this or that won't hurt you" is the lie he so smoothly told me. Relax, it's been a long hard day, you deserve a break. You name it. I have heard the many lies that he uses. More often than I care to admit to you. But drink I did. And drink. And drink. I bought the lies of Satan for a long time until the Truth of the Lord of Redemption spoke to me and saved me from myself. Every weakness toward that tool from hell was removed from me praise, God!!

I shared this with you because this portion of the scripture cried out to me about the power of the abuse of alcohol. It has destroyed kings and kingdoms and divided families. It has left in its wake a host of broken people searching endlessly for forgiveness and not even understanding that they really are forgiven. In Christ, they are indeed totally and wholly forgiven and accepted into His family. And that is what matters.

My prayer for each of us is that the wonderful redemptive love of our Lord and Savior Jesus Christ, be closer to us than the beating of our hearts. No one can hurt me anymore and I will no longer hurt myself. You see, I am indeed redeemed.

Chapter 9

As we continue on in Esther 1:16, we get a closer look at the "All the Kings men." Or at least at the outspoken one: Memucan. It would seem that he is an advisor that is closer than some of the others since he gives the king an earful of his thoughts regarding Queen Vashti.

As I said earlier, Queen Vashti has committed three very serious offenses. She has usurped the authority of a man, she has refused the authority of her husband, and most seriously for anyone, she has denied a request (command) from her king. Any one of these offenses could have and should have brought instant death to the offender. The question in my mind, again, is why did the king turn to his advisors and ask *them* what to do?

In a matter of moments, or as long as it took the poor shaking eunuch to deliver the message, the temperature in the garden has changed. Gone are the merry men of Persia and their drinking and partying. Gone is the over the top king, trying to prove how great his empire was. Gone is the talk of war and strategy. In its place is a simmering anger towards a woman who has cast doubt on the king and his mighty kingdom.

It doesn't really matter why Vashti refused to come to the garden. What matters is she did. In this situation, cool heads might have prevailed. You know, the advisors could have come to the king's aid and kept the whole thing under wraps. It is not like the eunuch came out from the women's quarters with a bullhorn and made the grave announcement for all to hear. But quiet reserve doesn't seem to be this king's strong suit does it. And so, his close advisor, Memucan, jumps at the chance to give his two cents worth to the king.

I had to agree with his assessment (vs.16) that the queen had indeed "wronged" the king. But as he continues in his speech, I was baffled, almost humorously I must admit, that his first and only concern seemed to be that there would be some kind of uprising with the other "women so that they will despise their own husbands." Shouldn't his first concern be for the kingdom that he served and not his own "happy hearth and home?" Obviously Memucan had some personal "home life" issues that he was dealing with and this was a perfect opportunity to take care of them.

Strength in numbers is what King Ahasuerus needs. He needs his army and his leaders behind him as he works his magic to convince them to go to war with Greece. He is desperately seeking to keep the facade of a happy balance. A true politician. This was certainly not the time for a revolt from anyone. But from the women???? I kept thinking and thinking, why did Memucan declare that the kingdom would practically fall apart (or at least his household) if the other "noble ladies" didn't see an immediate and harsh response from the king to the queen? In all reality, this was an issue from a husband to a wife. Have you wondered about that?

It is not like the women of the court had any rights besides the ones granted to them from their husbands. They could be "put out to pasture" at any time the men got tired of them. They didn't have a say in the comings or goings of their husbands, much less, input into how the provinces were run. Why then does Memucan spend the next few minutes convincing the king that he needs to do something and do something quickly?

Control. The running of a kingdom, the organizing of world affairs, and the conquering power behind it must at all cost have a united force. If the rest of the kingdom got wind that there was an apparent breach in authority between the king and any of his servants, his ability to lead, in their eyes would drop. If the king couldn't control his own wife, how could he possibly rule an empire as vast and prominent as Persia? Memucan knew the words to use and use them he did.

And so Memucan suggests that the mighty king issue a royal decree that Vashti be removed as the queen of Persia. In Persian law, once a decree was made, not even the king could revoke it. It is a done deal for all time. Now mind you, he could have made the suggestion that Vashti be hung from the gallows and paraded around the citadel for all to see. But he didn't. Read verse 20 and see if you notice what I did. Memucan is more concerned that the women of the kingdom "great and small" honor their husbands. Oh, to be able to sit down at *his* dinner table with him and his wife. She might tell us more about where his heart and mind is.

But the response pleased the king, and a royal decree was written up and sent out to all of the provinces. And just so there would be no misunderstanding how these ladies were to act towards their husbands, the letters were sent personally in all of the different languages of the kingdom. Memucan was going to cover all of the bases here.

I kept wondering (you know how I tend to wander in my wonderings), why Memucan responded in the way he did. My conclusion is once again control and the intoxicating effect that it has on people. In order to have power you must have the ability to be able to lead others and their lives. Obviously, the women of Memucan's household didn't care much for his style of "leadership" and maybe this was a thorn in his side. If he couldn't control his own household, how would he ever rule a large empire? Oh, wait. Did I just make the suggestion that Memucan might have had an ulterior motive here? Like taking over the rule of Persia someday? Who knows really? I do know this, though, people who desire power will normally stop at nothing to get it.

We end this portion of scripture with the royal decree being sent to all of the provinces in the kingdom. All 127 provinces. From India to Ethiopia. To all households. To all wives. And Queen Vashti? Well, she won't be put to death, but she will be removed from the royal palace. Where she goes and what she does is another study in itself. But for now, the king is without a queen.

Chapter 10

Chapter 2 begins with the words, "After these things..." Within scripture, especially at the beginning of a new chapter or verse, there are a couple of things to pay attention to. When you see words like "after these things" or "therefore," you have to stop and look at what the "therefore is there for." It is the writer's way of reminding us that the previous verses will play a part in the next section. So we need to ask ourselves, *what* things have happened?

The king has been hosting a six month feast and party. He has spent countless hours manipulating the leaders, wining and dining them so to speak, in order that they stand with him in his decision to go and conquer Greece. His purpose, as we have pointed out in earlier lessons, is to eventually take over and control the entire world. Part of his reasoning is, of course, world domination. But the other part, the part that burns deep within him, is revenge. Both reasons are fuel for his burning desire for wealth and power. When we left chapter 1 the party had abruptly come to an end. If you didn't know to look at the words "after these things" and see what things were being referred to, you might assume that the writer is referring to the proclamation about the queen. But, if you do some research on the timeline, you will see the activities to which the writer is referring.

Time has indeed passed since the garden party. About three years. The king had used these years for preparations for the invasion of Greece that would begin in the spring of 480 BC. During these few years, he strategically used the time wisely. He had a canal dug through the Peninsula of Mount Athos and built an enormous bridge across Hellesport. You see, the quantity of soldiers in the king's possession was vast. But quantity doesn't always mean QUALITY. Although the sheer number of soldiers is unmistakably huge, you can't always win a war with numbers. King Ahasuerus had the numbers, but the soldiers were ill-trained when it came to individual knowledge about battle. They worked in "team" fashion, but they were soundly beat because the Greek soldiers were trained to think individually as well as in teams. Sheer numbers couldn't compare to this kind of training.

King Ahasuerus traveled to the battlefield with two well-known advisors, Demaratus, who was a well known exiled Spartan king, and Artemisia, the Queen of Halicarnassus. Go ahead, say *that* title three times rapidly. When her father, King Lygdamis died, she succeeded him as queen and made a name for herself with King Ahasuerus during the naval battle of Salamis. I read some of the history about her and I must say, her talent as a naval commander was pretty impressive. It was Artemisia that convinced Ahasuerus to return to his homeland during the battle. You see, they were not faring very well, and it had reached a dangerous point for him to stay with the fleet and the troops. So, back home he went.

It wasn't long after his departure that the battle came to an end. You see, although the Persian Empire had the manpower, they didn't have the power of the man. Individual training had not been given, so unless the foot soldiers were able to attack in mass, their quantity was no rival for the quality that the smaller Greek army had. The Persian troops were completely beaten at their own game and sent packing with the yell of "Retreat!"

And so, King Ahasuerus returns home. To the beautiful and majestic palace. To the plush gardens. To a place where his every wish was fulfilled and his every need met. So why then does the very first verse of this chapter say, "After these things, when the wrath of King Ahasuerus was appeased, he remembered Vashti, and what she had done, and what had been decreed against her?" Hum. It is not like it is the next day, friends. A long time had elapsed since that fateful night in the garden. I wonder why it is that the first writing in the new chapter begins this way.

Have you ever thrown a good old fashioned hissy fit and then once you were calmed down and looked around, you thought to yourself, "Oh, no... I think I may have made a mistake." Well, I am thinking that might be exactly what the king is thinking.

Chapter 11

We rejoin King Ahasuerus in chapter 2 of Esther as he is moping around his palace feeling lonely and dejected. The realization of his current situation has hit, and hit him hard. Not only was he sent packing back to his citadel in Shushan, but when he arrives, he looks around and the jewel in his crown, Queen Vashti, is no longer there. Now, I want you to understand that scripture does not tell us where she went or what she did after her banishment. There are some historians that believe that she became known by the Greek name, *Amestris* and was the mother of Artaxerxes II. Remember from our previous study that some thought she may have either been pregnant at the time or had recently given birth to Ahasuerus' son, and that was a reason she refused to dance.

I have thought long and hard about Esther 2:1. Why did the king give thought to Vashti? Was he lonely? Did he need the company of a woman? He didn't need to look too far for that, if that was the case. He had well over 300 wives. Why not just send one of his faithful eunuchs to go fetch another one for him? Obviously, there is more to this than meets the eye. I am in no way a big history scholar, but I keep thinking that the "role" of the queen, including her tasks within the kingdom and her importance as the Royal female leader, may have had something to do with it. She may very well have had diplomatic responsibilities, much like our "first women" in government do. She may have been responsible for social engagements that define the kingdom and the power and might of the ruling king. This was not just a case of being the proverbial "eye candy" for the empire. The queen had responsibilities, to be sure, but remember that Vashti was a Babylonia princess. Her alliance with *her* people needed to be nurtured. Without her, the risk of alienation of the Babylonians was now a real threat to the kingdom.

It is also important to remember that even the king himself cannot change what he decreed. This is indeed one of the most baffling laws that I have tried to understand. But, if you think about it, it does make sense. It would cause the ruling king to be very careful and very select in the decrees that he made, wouldn't you say? He would think long and hard about them first, right? Or at least he should, because as we learned from the previous chapter, he didn't think it through when he disposed of Queen Vashti.

So, it is decided that messengers would go to each of the 127 provinces and bring back "beautiful young virgins" for a kind of ancient day beauty contest. In writing this, I had to stop and ask myself a question. How in the world do you send messengers out to find and bring back virgins? Beautiful ones at that? I am not sure what their messaging system was back then, but I would venture to say that "email" and "snail mail" were not around yet. This meant that these messengers jumped on either a horse or a camel and took off to go deliver the decree to the provinces.

Let's get some perspective here. The land mass of the Persian Empire was 7.5 million kilometers. Not sure what a kilometer is compared to a mile? Well, let me share this little tidbit with you. The total contiguous land mass of the Empire equals 4.7 million square miles!!! And I complain about walking to the mailbox!!! Since there were no cars, motorcycles or even bicycles at this time, the mode of transportation was the trusty camel or horse. Now, if a camel can travel about 30 miles per day and a horse, depending on the size of the rider and the terrain can travel about 30-60 miles, it is going to take MORE than just a few days to make the rounds to the provinces. And can you also say "Saddle sores???" I must admit that I hadn't given much thought to the "social network" that these people used, but I am sure Facebook would have come in quite handy right about then!!

Regardless of how long it would take, the king had issued the command and off went the messengers on their quest. Miles and miles and MILES were traveled. Days and days and DAYS of hot sun as saddle weary men rode from place to place seeking to fill the order and bring back beautiful young virgins for the king. They went from door to door, neighborhood to neighborhood, family to family, seeking to find the replacement for Queen Vashti.

Oh, it might be an honor to become the new queen, if you were of Persian descent. But what if you are not Persian? Or, what happens if the king doesn't like what he sees? What happens to the young girls who are no longer virgins once they spend time with the king? They become just another object or part of the collection in the harem and that is where they live for the rest of their lives. Heartbreaking to me. But think about this question for a minute. What if you just happen to be a beautiful young Jewish girl? Do you hide under the bed when the messengers come to your house? Do you run for the hills and try to hide until the search is over? Or, is there even a hiding place to go to where you won't be found?

Chapter 12

As we continue on in Chapter 2, the king has sent out his messengers to find a new queen (v.1-4). Now, once again, I must remind you of the great undertaking that this task presents to those camel riding messengers. The distance from the citadel in Shushan to the western portion of the empire is 1600 miles. To the eastern border of the empire from Shushan is 1200 miles. The entire land mass is equal to about 4.7 MILLION square miles. If a camel travels 30 miles a day- well... you get what I am trying to say here? This was no easy task and it certainly didn't get done in just a few days. Biblical history in its entirety is so important that I want to make certain that we understand just what was involved here and what this mighty, yet lonely king asked of his servants.

At the same time that the messengers were off scouring the towns for the perfect offering for their king, we are introduced to Mordecai (v.5). The writer takes the time to list for us the family lineage of Modecai. Why? Well, he will play an important role in the rest of the book, and so we need to understand not only "who" he is, but who his *family* is to get a better picture. Kish was Mordecai's great-grandfather, and he was part of the Babylonian deportation by King Nebuchadnezzar. This was back in about 605 BC, after the Babylonian Empire was defeated by the Medo-Persian Empire, even more Jewish descendants were moved to other places within the territory. Kish would represent a Jewish family lineage for Mordecai, and the family can be traced back to Saul's father (1 Sam. 9:1). Kish was captured along with Jeconiah, the King of Judah. Hadassah, or as we call her, Esther, was raised by Mordecai, her uncle. According to verse 7 she was taken in by him and raised after her parents died. We don't know for sure how or even where they died. All we know is that she came and lived with Mordecai in Shushan.

The events of the book of Esther take place during the first return of the Jews after the 70 years of captivity in Babylon (approx. 538 BC), and the second return led by Ezra in 458 BC. It is important to note that the "return" would be going back to Jerusalem. At the time of this writing there were still millions of Israelites that had chosen NOT to return to their homeland, Mordecai was one of them. This fact (the fact that they remained out of their chosen land) helps us to understand that they were not in the will of God. Maybe it can help clarify other parts of the book for us. If you turn back in your Bible two books, you can read the accounts of Ezra concerning the decree of freedom given by Cyrus the King of Babylon. Also, on another side note (and you know I love to share tidbits of information with you) this is the same palace where Daniel resided after he was held captive. I must admit, I wasn't aware of that. Were you? And... this is the same palace that Nehemiah will seek permission from to go and rebuild the walls of Jerusalem. So as you can see, this little book holds a key to understanding the ongoing redemptive power and love of our God. Even though it seems like His chosen children have forgotten Him, He is still close by watching out for them.

Many commentaries dwell on the fact that God is never mentioned within these 167 verses. I don't dwell on what is NOT there, my friends. I look deeply to see what IS there. God loves His people and uses the circumstances surrounding them to carry out His will. If you believe that we serve a sovereign God, and I *know* we do, then look closely at the heart of Him who is in control of these circumstances. They might not be offering up prayers and praises to Him, but that doesn't mean that He is not with them. He is there. In every situation. In every decision. In every breath they take. HE IS THERE!!!

Have you ever wandered far from the Lord? Have you ever traveled to places like Moab, knowing full well you shouldn't go there, and yet you find yourself lulled there by deception? Our own self will. We talked about my travels to Moab in our study on Ruth, remember? I have traveled there and then had the audacity to blame God for the misfortune that came from my travels. The honest Christians that I know (and love for their honesty) are the first to admit that their own "lands of Moab" are never quite out of reach. There is this sense of urgency almost to have our own way, make our own path, and do "what is right in our own eyes" kind of attitude. Can't you see that in your own life sometimes? I know I sure can. Well, maybe, just maybe, that self-preservation kind of attitude is what is happening here in the citadel of Shushan.

We can't second guess the reason that Mordecai stayed in Shushan instead of heading to Jerusalem when he had the chance. We just can't do that. If God wanted us to know the reason, it would have been written within the verses for all to see and understand. Since it is not, I won't speculate as to why he made the choice to stay. But his decision to stay is a God-send for his people, isn't it? And that, for me is the first "quiet" reference to God in this book. For without the intervening of God within the disobedience of Mordecai, we would have lost the nation of Israel. So you see, I don't believe that God isn't present in this book. I believe that *His* will and *His* voice were heard and acted upon by Mordecai. In fact, I believe that God is throughout this whole book. And I know that we will come to that same conclusion when we are done.

Chapter 13

In the last chapter we met Mordecai, Esther's cousin. Remember, she is Mordecai's uncle, Abihail's daughter. Her parents were deceased, and he took her in and raised her as his own daughter. Now, I started to think about her parents and Mordecai's family too. The verses don't tell us that they have other close family in Shushan with them, so it is probably safe to assume that they don't. It is the two of them, trying to fit into a society where they don't really belong. Hmm. Have we heard of another family that tried this before? Anyone remember Elimelech and Naomi?

I consider myself to be a thoughtful person. Anyone who knows me would have to agree. I am FULL of thoughts all day long. Some good and some... well... I have already admitted my journey to Moab, so no use going into detail about bad thoughts now, is there? Suffice it to say any thought of chocolate, when I KNOW I am not supposed to have it... well... you know how it is. Anyway, as I was saying, I am a very thought filled person. I think all day long. My mind wonders and wanders about the people, places and things that I have come in contact with during the day. As I study each day, there will be certain verses that catch my attention. As I continued in the study, it was Mordecai that caught my attention.

As you know already, Mordecai was Esther's older cousin. How much older I don't know. But he was in a position to care for her as a parental figure. Let's read Esther 2:5-7 together and see if you notice the same thing that I did. Do you see it???? Look closely again. As many times as I have read this section of the book, I had missed it. Hadassah.

Hadassah is Esther's Hebrew name. Look at verse 7 again. "And Mordecai had brought up Hadassah, that is Esther, for she had neither father nor mother." And this is where my wondering thoughts started wandering through commentaries. The very first reference to Esther is by her original HEBREW name. And yet, where is the Hebrew name for Mordecai within these verses? He is always referred to as Mordecai. Well, once again, I got to thinking. Remember, I am thoughtful. So I did some checking into our dear cousin Mordecai, and I must tell you, I was pretty surprised by what I found out. Let's get a closer look at him, shall we?

I did some research on the name Mordecai, it seems the name is Persian, not Hebrew. Now, I did not know that. I just assumed, for some reason, that it was his Hebrew name since he was Jewish. I thought that because the verses clearly told us that Esther's name was really Hadassah. I thought that she was given a Persian name since she married a Persian king. But a Hebrew name for Mordecai is not given. In checking what his Persian name might mean, I found it could mean "Warrior" or "Little Man." But, more interestingly, the name refers to Marduk, one of the gods of the Babylonians and literally means "follower, servant or devotee" of this god Marduk. Now what is in a name, you say? Plenty, in this case.

Now I know that even Daniel was assigned a new name. I understand that. But he didn't identify himself with it. He stayed true to his own name and heritage even while he was serving the Babylonian king. But here, the writer never calls Mordecai anything other than... well... Mordecai. And if there is a remote possibility that the writer of the book is Mordecai, then why not use his given name? There must be a reason, and I intend to wonder and then wander until I find out for us.

Within the Talmud, Mordecai is referred to by his Hebrew name of Bilshan. Hmm... where I have seen THAT name before? Let's mosey on back in our Bibles to the Book of Ezra 2:2. That family name is used in the group of people that came with Zerubbabel back to Jerusalem. Now, mind you, one of my Bible references says that the "Nehemiah" and "Mordecai" mentioned in these verses are not the same men as mentioned in Nehemiah and Esther. Interesting since the name Mordecai isn't used in this verse. It is Bilshan. So why even put that in there? Unless, of course, that THIS Bilshan is somehow related to our own Mordecai?????

I also found that the name Mordecai could have been used as a nickname. Now I have to say, I have been called a lot of nicknames growing up, as I am sure most of us have. Mine were things like "Curly Girly" because I had naturally curly hair. But as we mature, we don't use names like that anymore. Especially if they are negative, like "Marduk follower." Why would he want to be identified with Marduk? Why not immediately use a name that represents who he is NOW, for goodness sake? Even if it meant "Little Man," I would still most definitely change it. Wouldn't you?

Quite baffling, isn't it? But that is the blessing of scripture, I think. It causes us to become thoughtful. We start thinking and looking and looking and thinking, and pretty soon we wonder through our wanderings and find great things and knowledge to be had and used. I do so love the scriptures, don't you? Although I don't have any firm answer as to the "name," it does give me cause to wander just a tiny bit more. Hey, I know. Why don't you wonder about it and then wander around and see what you come up with.

Chapter 14

As I said before, had my nickname had a negative connotation to it, like the name Mordecai had, I very well would have tried to change it or tried to be given another nickname, but he didn't so... Mordecai it is.

I want us to get a good picture in our minds about what is going on at the citadel right now. The young girls are beginning to be brought into the town and housed at the women's quarters. Imagine for a moment how the city must look and sound right about now. You know as well as I do that not every young maiden has her heart set on being brought to the palace for this beauty contest. And it really is a beauty contest. Some of these young women may have had young men in their lives that were now left behind. Their life, as they once knew it, was over, never to return. Once a part of the king's harem, always a part of the king's harem. There may very well have been parents jumping for joy at the chance that their daughter might become the Queen of Persia, but at the same time, I would say a good majority of them realized the odds against that happening. There must have been a great number of broken hearted parents mourning the loss of their daughters.

The Persian kings were known for their collections. Gold, silver, gems, land, livestock, women. That's right I said *women*. Possessing things and then showing them off was a great pleasure for King Ahasuerus, as we learned from the previous verses in chapter 1. Women were a dime a dozen and were taken by force if necessary to live out their days in the palace harem. On this quest, a decree had been issued to bring back beautiful young virgins. As the groups arrive, they are handed over to the eunuch Hegai, who will have the responsibility for their "preparations".

In verse 8 we see that Esther too, is taken to the citadel and handed off to Hegai. Once again, let's notice the word "taken." Taken is just that folks, *taken*. There is not a reference that I can find that even makes the suggestion that this was her idea or that she went willingly or that Mordecai suggested it. She, like many, many other young women, was taken by the king's decree to the palace. This situation speaks to me yet again of the "hand of God" within these verses. He is in   the background,   quietly,   yet   completely   and compassionately guiding the situation. Look closely at verse 9 and maybe you will see His work as I did. Esther found favor from Hegai. Do you remember when Ruth was gleaning in the fields and she found favor with Boaz? A person who didn't need to show another favor did, because the sovereign God orchestrated it. Amazing, isn't it, that even though His name is not mentioned within the verses of this book, He is still in control.

Hegai perceives a quality in Esther that he acts upon. Not only is she beautiful, but she is described as "lovely" too (vs 7). Beautiful is her physical attribute and lovely is the condition of her heart. This is what Hegai finds favor in. She possesses a natural caring heart. She isn't caught up in her physical beauty folks. If she would have strolled into the women's quarters demanding this and requiring that, I don't think Hegai would have been willing to help her like he does. But here, he sees a quality in her that he does not notice in anyone else and he acts upon it. He readily gives her extra things to make certain that she is well equipped for the task at hand. And, if that is not enough, he supplies her with seven "choice" maidens to assist her. What a blessing he has bestowed on her when she didn't even ask for one. Can you see the beginning of redemption happening here??????

We serve an awesome God. One who knows the good and the bad. One who sees every single situation that we are put it, and in His glorious might, works all things for the good for those that love Him. Hope is found within these verses. Hope for the young maiden Hadassah. Hope for the nation of Israel. Hope for you and for me. Do you need hope today? Is your life full of doubt and fear? Do you feel like you are paddling upstream all by yourself? Then cast your eyes heavenward, my friend. Look up and bask in the glorious rays of the Son. He is there. He is willing. He is able to put your heart at rest.

Chapter 15

As we rejoin our study in chapter 2, we can see that the women's quarter of the citadel is a busy place. For the next year, these young maidens will be pampered and prepared for their "one night with the King." That's right... I said ONE YEAR. Twelve months of beauty treatments and preparations. Aromatic baths, hair styling, facials, makeup lessons. Who doesn't like to be pampered?

Although each of the young maidens receives what she needs, Hegai, the custodian of all of the women, has taken a special shine to Esther. She possesses the quality that he thinks his king will see and appreciate. As any good employee will do, he acts upon it and takes her under his wing. Remember, he too is out to please the king. Failure of any kind is frowned upon and could cost him not only his job, but his life.

Verse 10 tells us that Esther had not revealed her people or family. There are two distinct words here that I want us to think about. People and family. Mordecai has instructed her to remain silent about her heritage. Her Jewish heritage. Scripture doesn't tell us why this is, but for whatever reason, he feels that she should not divulge that she is Jewish. So, it would stand to reason that she (and he for that matter) are not openly observing their Jewish faith and traditions. Perhaps they are acting the part of, "when in Rome... do as the Romans do?" In other words, they have chosen to fit in with the crowd.

Have you ever done that? Fitting in with the crowd is a temptation that we all face each day. As Christians we live and work in a sinful world full of people that want to bring us down to their sinful level. They look down their noses at us for trying to live as Christ would have us live. The workplace is full of people with a "dog-eat-dog" attitude and a "show no mercy" work ethic. It is difficult, to say the least, to maintain the standard of excellence that God desires for us when each day we are bombarded with sinful people laying traps for us to slip up and fail. Philippians 4:13 tells us that we "can do all things through Christ who strengthens me." Hold on to that verse friends. When the workday is filled with the sinful challenges from those around you, know in your heart that Christ will indeed give you the strength to get through it.

In reading verse 11, I realized something about Mordecai that I hadn't really noticed before. He had compassion in his heart for Esther and for her situation at the citadel. It says, "he paced in front of the women's court." Each day he went there to check on Esther. Have you ever paced before? Have you ever walked the floor at night praying for a sick friend? Have you paced back and forth at a hospital waiting for news of a loved one? Have you ever walked back and forth and back and forth, wearing a path in the carpet because your heart was so heavy with worry? This is what we see here.

Mordecai knows that the fate of his cousin is not guaranteed. Nowhere in these verses do we see it recorded that Mordecai had received a vision from the Lord that Esther would become the queen. He is just as human in his feelings and concern for her as we would be if this was happening to one of our daughters. He paced. Each day. Back and forth. Alone. Worried. For twelve very long months he paced. That speaks to me of the heart of Mordecai. A genuine concern for Esther that I hadn't seen before. Can't you just feel his anguish?

The decision for Esther to be a part of this "beauty contest" was not theirs. It was decided by force when the messengers went into town to gather young maidens for the harem. Some of the young girls may very well have been from an area where there was much poverty, so this could have been viewed as a "way out." And then, of course, you would have had the parents that just knew in their heart that their daughter would be chosen to be queen because after all she is the prettiest girl in the world. But we know, that it was the sovereign God we serve, who orchestrated the where, when and how of Esther becoming the next queen.

Once again, I argue with anyone that says that God is NOT in this book. As we get further along I am sure that you will agree that He is indeed there, woven into the lives of Esther and Mordecai. These two unlikely cousins will bring about the saving of a nation through the working hand of the God they serve. Oh they may not be praying to Him openly. They may not be serving Him as they should. They may not even recognize the plan that He has for them. But isn't that true of many of us in our own lives? Haven't you ever "set God aside" for awhile? Haven't you ever tried to blend in for the sake of blending in, just so that the old boat wouldn't be rocked? I know that I have.

My prayer for each of us is that we see the places that we go, you know the Moab journeys that we take, and recognize the times that we too have strayed away from the path the Lord has for us. The Lord used this situation to bring two of His children back into a redeeming relationship with Him. He wants the same for you and for me!!

Chapter 16

"Each young woman's turn came to go to King Ahasuerus after she had completed twelve months of preparation, according to the *regulations* for the women" vs. 12. When I saw the word "regulation" I immediately thought to myself that this tradition, this gathering of young maidens, must have happened in the past. Why? Because there is a precedent to follow. There are rules. In other words, gathering young women for the sensual pleasure of the king is not a new thing. You only have rules and regulations in place, if the situation has happened before or will happen again in the future. Interesting, isn't it?

In seeking out the reason behind the regulations for this procedure, I began to understand why this was even necessary in this instance. The women that were housed in the harem were used only as the king saw fit to use them. In other words, their time with the king could be few and far between. He might only be with them once the entire time they were there. It was totally up to him. But this occasion, this particular situation, was far different. The king was going to name a new queen. The stakes were different and the bar had been raised.

The time spent under the care of Hegai was divided into two six-month periods. The first six months the women were treated with aromatic baths and oil of myrrh. Myrrh has a fragrance, but most likely in this setting, it would have been used for its medicinal purposes. Actually, I was quite amazed at all the ailments for which myrrh could have been used. It is still used today. The most common uses are for sore throats, stomach ailments, skin problems, and infections. Myrrh is also used as an astringent and as an anti-parasitic.

How many of you remember the story of "Cinderella?" Can't you just almost picture our friend Hegai as the little chubby mouse that was desperate to help Cinderella win the heart of Prince Charming? He joyfully went about his business collecting the beautiful beads that the kindly birds would sew on Cinderella's gown. Another picture that comes to my mind is that of Rex Harrison in the classic movie, "My Fair Lady" as he repeated the words, "The rain in Spain falls mainly on the plain" to the breathtakingly beautiful, yet not-quite-ready for prime-time Audrey Hepburn. Each of these heartwarming scenarios is one of someone giving of themselves to another person in the sincere hope of assisting that person achieve their goal. Hegai personally gives freely to Esther in the hope that she will be recognized by the king, as "The One."

Once the young women have spent the first six months being physically cleansed, they are then ready for the next six months of beauty treatments. We need to understand that part of the reason for the first six months is to clear up any medical issues and make certain that the women don't bring any type of disease to the king. Once they have passed this standard, they are on to the next round of spa treatments and court etiquette. After all, the search was for a new queen. Oh, but not just *any* queen. She would be THE Queen. The Queen of Persia. The standards and expectations that Ahasuerus had were high. Our friend Hegai had his work cut out for him.

I would like to point out one more thing today that I noticed in my reading. Look back at verse 9 for just a moment. Remember how we had discussed that Mordecai and Esther were not observing their Jewish tradition and roots? Well, I kept thinking about that. I looked up the word that is used in that verse (allowance) and the Hebrew word is "manah." It has to do with food. Unlike the "manna" that God provided for the Israelites when they wandered in the wilderness, this word is used to mean an allotment of food or a special food. The NIV says, "Immediately he (Hegai) provided her (Esther) with her beauty treatments and special food." I must say that caught my eye and made me curious as to what it could mean. Why is food even brought up in this section. It is not like Esther could have placed an order for only the types of foods that she liked. She, as well as all of the other women, would have no choice as to what was served to them. I think what we see is that Hegai made sure that she was given the best of the best even where the food was concerned. The freshest fruits, vegetables, and meats to aid in her beauty regimen.

The next six months are spent dabbling in the art of cosmetics and perfumes. Not all women look good in the same colors of clothes or make-up, nor smell good wearing certain perfumes. All of us are different, and it was up to Hegai and his crew to utilize the natural beauty of each of these maidens, to enhance it where they deemed necessary. Eye shadow, color from crushed berries would be applied and then reapplied to enhance the eye color. Rosy red cheeks were created from the natural color from such things as pomegranates. Long silky hair that has been brushed to a shining glory, delicately and seductively styled to bring out the shape of their faces. Lip color to shade and highlight the perfect smile. Fragrant plant oils used as perfume were dabbed on here and there, so that when a woman made her entrance into the king's chambers, her delicate yet delightful aroma would be noticed by him. They were taught how to walk, talk, and "be" the queen.

Scripture paints such a wonderful picture of the people, places and happenings within the writings. Some of the words move me to tears. Some of the words bring a quiet comfort to my weary soul. Some of them even make me chuckle at the circumstances in which the people find themselves. And some, like today, bring me a hope and a joy. I pray each of you see the invisible hand of God as He directs the circumstances and outcome of the lives of Esther, Mordecai and even old King Ahasuerus.

God had a plan then, and He has a plan now. For you. For me.

Chapter 17

As we continue in our study, we have come to a sort of crossroads for me personally. I must admit that I am a romantic. I kept reading these verses over and over again to find the romance, the part where the bells were ringing in the great palace announcing the wedding of the king. But I couldn't hear them, nor could I read them in-between the lines. My human heart ached for a picture-perfect day for Esther, didn't yours?

In looking back over the years, I can recall with great joy wedding days within our family. The planning and the fussing. The laughter and the tears. All of it with loving family gathered around on that special day. The hopes and dreams of the young couple becoming a reality as they stand side by side, professing their love and commitment to each other. The entire congregation of family and friends cheers for the new married couple as they practically dance down the aisle on the way to the reception party.

It has only taken the writer a mere 36 verses to get to this part of the story. Hmm... Now I know for sure that a woman could NOT have written this book. As I said in the previous lesson about the "garden party," a woman would have written down the sights and sounds of the party, and all of the guests. The dresses, the jewelry, the makeup, the hairstyles. We girls are very much into the details of such affairs. How could it be possible that a wedding day, a day of great celebration for the King of Persia, could pass by the writer with almost no mention at all?

In verse 16 we find that in the tenth month, which is called Tebeth, of the seventh year of Ahasuerus' reign, Esther is presented to him and finds favor with him. Once again, it is important to note, that Esther finds favor with the king, much like she did with Hegai. Her calm, dignified spirit, not just her physical beauty, is what the king sees in her and what attracts him to her. In verse 17 it says "the king loved Esther more than the other women." We must be careful not to assume that this is saying that he was "in" love with her. Being "in" love with someone takes time to nurture and cultivate the relationship. He loved what he saw in her beauty and found it more favorable than the others. Even though I have read this book many, many times, I still wanted to feel like he cherished her and loved her deeply.

Once King Ahasuerus sees Esther his mind is made up. She will be the new queen. He personally places the royal crown of Persia on her head and declares her his queen. Notice that the writer adds these words "instead of Vashti." A small part of me asked if this was put in to remind us of the fate of Vashti in her denial of the king, or perhaps the writer knew that the king had indeed had feelings for Vashti. Or, maybe the writer himself was aligned with Vashti and he felt the ache of the loss of her in the kingdom. We may never know why those few words were included.

There are times when I read the scriptures about people and I want to put my own feelings into the scenario. I want them to feel a certain way, act a certain way, and have the outcome be the one that I want. That is part of our human nature. We want what we want when we want it. But this account is not about feelings. This account is not about the big wedding day in Persia. It is about the faithful God that we serve. The God that Mordecai and Esther's family had at one time also served. His faithfulness to His people must not be blanketed by my own human emotions for a happy ending. Prince Charming and Cinderella are nowhere to be found in these verses, and I can't put something into God's word that is not there.

Maybe that is why the writer of this book left out the details. So that you and I wouldn't just see the Pomp and Circumstance of this royal wedding and lose sight of the reason it was taking place. It is the workings of a sovereign God with a sovereign plan for His people carefully placing Mordecai and Esther in just the right place at just the right time, or as Mordecai will later say "...For such a time as this."

Chapter 18

Wedding day in Shushan. A girl. A king. The beginning of a time in history when the Lord Almighty Himself would motivate, captivate, and initiate the ruler of the Persian Empire to move in a way that most would have thought impossible. But as we know, "For with God nothing shall be impossible," Luke 1:37.

I still must admit that I have looked long and hard to find and then write about the sights and sounds of the wedding day that takes place within these verses. I wanted romance. I longed for the details of the glamorous gowns. The picture of the intricately crafted crown placed upon Esther's head as she solemnly and yet, with quiet dignity, accepts her role as the new Queen of Persia. A delicately hand-woven silk gown so breathtaking in its color and allure, that it has never met its match. Jewelry so glittery and over the top that no other kingdom could have possibly come close to the magnitude of such finery. A table of the finest foods, set before a mighty king and his court, so delectable that countless other feasts of other empires would have paled in comparison to any of the feasts they would have had in the past, present or future of this time. And all of it, all of it done, to honor Hadassah, now and forever known as Esther. But alas, it was nowhere to be found. These are just the wishes of my own romantic heart.

King Ahasuerus followed the Zoroastrian religion. This is the religion of the Magi who came to seek out and worship the newborn King of kings, Jesus. They also, were followers of the Zoroastrian religion and were astrologers. The wedding of the King of Persia would have indeed had many ceremonial rituals that would have followed the guidelines of this religion. The religion itself is still practiced by some today and there are many writings about it if you care to go and check them out.

I have thought many thoughts and wondered and then wandered. How could this have been possible? This whole scenario of Esther and Mordecai, in a place where they shouldn't have been, placed now in a situation that seems almost too impossible to overcome, made me think back to our friends Elimelech and Naomi from the story of Ruth, who moved to a land where they shouldn't have been and found themselves in a situation that also seemed impossible. I must admit to you all, as I readily do, that I am sometimes more analytical than I should be. I go searching for answers to the "what, where, why and how" of the situation. Why did Mordecai choose to stay in Shushan in the first place? And why, when the decree from the king went out for a new queen, didn't he grab his young and beautiful cousin by the hand and flee to the safety of Jerusalem?

Have you ever been in this kind of a situation? Where your choices of what and where you are have brought you to a place of confusion and fear? Not knowing if you actually are in God's will or if it is just your own desires taking precedence over what you should be doing? I know that for me, it happens much too often. It reminds me of Paul when he writes about wanting so desperately to do the will of God and yet somehow not doing it. Our own will is so strong in its pull within our spirit that it is sometimes very difficult to discern what we should be doing. And yet, you find that when you are indeed in the will of the Lord, walking in the path that He has chosen for you, there is a peace that settles upon your soul and the weariness of "thinking" about it leaves you. When I feel peaceful, then I know that I am on the right path, don't you?

Maybe this is the kind of quiet peace that Esther felt on this most important day. She may not have known where the path would take her or why she was even on it, but there was a peace within her. We may not read about God within these verses, but He is indeed there. He is the guiding force behind the decisions that were made. Out of all of those young and beautiful girls, do you really think it was just happenstance that Esther was chosen? Not me. I believe with everything in me that we serve a sovereign God who, since the beginning of time, has been involved in the big plan of the world and all of its inhabitants. I rest assured each night because of that fact.

Chapter 19

As we begin today in 2:19, Esther is beginning her reign as the Queen of Persia, while Mordecai has taken on a position of authority at the king's gate. Remember from our study in Ruth that the city gate is the area where daily business and legal matters take place. It was where Boaz caught up with the other family member and requested to redeem Ruth. This area of the citadel serves the same purpose.

Although, in the previous verses Mordecai's occupation is not discussed, it seems now that he is a more prominent figure. Some commentary writers feel that after Esther became queen she elevated him to a position of good standing. He is now "within" the gate instead of "outside" the gate. Positionally speaking, his role in the Persian society has been upgraded. He is in a place where he most likely would not have been before. Close to the kings men.

Have you ever worked for a company during a transitional time when the upper management changes and new people are brought in? Oftentimes, the new leader will bring in his or her own management team to "revamp" the business. Leaders want people around them who will not only serve them, but be loyal to them. Businesses, households, and even kingdoms and societies can rise and be successful or fall and fail miserably depending upon the loyalty of those involved.

In 2:18 we read that King Ahasuerus had "made Esther queen instead of Vashti." Once again as he seems prone to do when he wants to celebrate things, he throws a huge party. "The Feast of Esther" is what the Bible calls it. Again we see that from far and wide, the officials are invited to attend. I just want to remind you that the kingdom is 4.7 million square miles. Just sending out notification/invitations could take a few weeks. But, as we recall from the kings decree for the virgins to be sent to him, the messengers are sent and the party is scheduled.

A holiday is declared throughout the many provinces, which some writers feel would mean that the king would not have taxed his subjects for a period of time. How long we don't know, but any tax relief would have been a welcome gift. But then scripture goes on to say that he gave gifts, "according to the generosity of the king". It made me think back to the garden party from the previous chapter and all of the golden goblets that were totally unique. Remember those? Some scholars feel that the goblets could have been a gift to each guest. Makes me wonder what special item he would have given to commemorate his wedding day.

It is now four years since Vashti has been in the palace. But that does not necessarily mean that she was forgotten. She may very well have had people in her corner that were loyal to her for whatever reason. Remember, she was a Babylonian princess and she would have been most likely sympathetic to those of that culture. To no longer have her in their corner, so to speak, might have angered them and made them resentful of the king and his new queen.

Has that ever happened to you? At work? At home? Or even at church? New people come in and kind of take over? You have done things a certain way for a long time and now, here they come wanting to change everything up. Do things THEIR way. It hurts your feelings doesn't it? Sometimes in our moment of weakness and when our feelings are hurt, we say or do things that may not be very, well... Christian-like. OK, let me be honest here for a minute. I will admit that when a situation arises like this and my feelings get hurt, I am not a very nice person. I lash out with words or even actions that more times than not, I later regret. Is anybody with me here? Why, oh why, are our feelings so *easily* hurt and yet so *difficult* to control??? Total opposites.

As we continue on into verse 21, we will meet two gatekeepers that seem to be experiencing just these kinds of feelings. Anger, frustration and even revenge. Why? I am not sure. But their emotions, their feelings, cause quite a stir in the kingdom.

Chapter 20

I truly believe that each and every time I read scripture something is shown to me that I can usually apply to my own life. Not that every verse has the disclaimer of "Nansii Downer, this is meant for you" put on it, but I do believe that what I need to see, hear, or learn can be found within most of the writings. Such is the case from this section of our lesson. Let's join the study at 2:21.

I have titled this section "Righteous Gossip." Someone hears something that someone else is saying and then... well... tells someone else. Now, some of you might say that these verses are not really gossip because gossip is, by definition, when you repeat something that may or may not be true or that would cause harm to another. Gossip can cause disunity, disharmony, and even disobedience. I think that each of us would agree to that, don't you? But what about a situation like Mordecai finds himself in? Let's explore this and see what we find out about Mordecai and perhaps ourselves.

As Mordecai is working the gate area, conducting the daily business, he happens to overhear a conversation between two of the king's trusted servants, Bigthan and Teresh. Let's stop right there a minute OK? Mordecai is working alongside these men. How he came to be there doesn't really matter, but it would seem that his new position was brought about after the wedding of his cousin to the king. In other words, this is a transitional, positional move. He is there, within earshot, because he has been moved there. So, the first thing I want us to think about is how this transition might make the "other" servants feel. Our human emotion is the driving force behind most of the things that we say and do.

Verse 21 says, "In those days, while Mordecai sat within the kings's gate, Bigthan and Teresh became furious and sought to lay hands on the king." What exactly were they furious about? The new queen, perhaps? Mordecai's new position at the gate, perhaps? Or just the general circumstances surrounding this kingdom? Any number of answers could fit here, you know? Scripture doesn't tell us the reason why because well, the *reason* for the anger isn't what is important here. It is the result of the feelings of anger that we are to focus on.

Have you ever been angry and said something that you really didn't mean to be taken literally? I know I have many times. Now mind you, I am in no way suggesting that Bigthan and Teresh didn't mean to follow through on their threat against the king. As we read further in the verses, we will see that the matter was investigated and found to be true. But what caught my attention, the lesson that the Lord was showing me, was that discernment is the greater part of valor.

If I had a nickel for every time I repeated something that shouldn't have been repeated, well... let's just say I could probably take a nice vacation with the change. Prov. 11:13 says, "A talebearer reveals secrets, but he who is of a faithful spirit conceals a matter." How faithful is my spirit? What good will my repeating a matter do? Will an innocent person be hurt by my misspoken words? Or worse, how will my words affect another person's life and reputation?

There have been many instances in the world around me when half-truths have been told and the outcome is devastating for those involved. Sometimes, as much as we would *wish* we could, we can never take the words back nor change the outcome. Accusations made or overheard and repeated have been and will continue to be a heartbreaking instance of a self-willed person who is definitely not using their "faithful spirit".

I have had to learn (and I admit that I am still learning) that silence is sometimes more than just "golden." It is called for. The Lord God Almighty did not place me here on His earth to be the great bearer of all messages for all people. As I have sought to find my spiritual gifts, I have yet to see one that designates me as being the "town crier." Through many tearful and tear-filled lessons I have come to the realization that sometimes a repeated matter is repeated simply for the pleasure of repeating it. OUCH !!

For whatever reason, the Lord in His mighty wisdom kept bringing me back to this painful lesson: Admitting that I have been wrong on many occasions and that I need to use the tools that He has so freely given me helps when dealing with overheard conversations.

Discernment... discernment... and then MORE discernment !!!

Now mind you, I am not saying that ALL things should be kept under wraps. I think you know me better than that. But I do say that each of us, when presented with a situation that calls for discernment needs to follow our heart and really "think" before we speak. And while you are at it... pray before you even start thinking !!! Ask the Lord's good guidance as to what you should do. He is faithful to those who love and serve Him......especially when we need his blessed discernment.

In the next chapter we will look a little closer to the situation with Bigthan, Teresh and Mordecai. This time in a whole new perspective.

Chapter 21

In looking at verses 21-23 of chapter 2, I would like to suggest another scenario for your consideration. I call this section "The Great Set-up." I would like to venture "outside" of the scripture lesson and venture "inside" our own lives for a moment. Bear with me and follow along, OK?

It's a calm and quiet morning at the gate. Mordecai, Teresh and Bigthan are conducting the business of the day and all the while, between the transactions, they are just kind of, well, chit-chatting. You know, that meaningless babbling back and forth that employees do while at work. Kind of like the days of the meetings at the water cooler. Monday mornings, employees would meet by the old water cooler to kind of catch up on their weekend adventures. Or......they would schmooze with each other and "share the news" about happenings within the office. Anyone who has worked in an office can relate to what I am talking about here.

Low and behold, and it seldom failed, someone would say something not so very pleasant about the boss. A little dig here and small jab there. Pretty soon, most everyone was chiming in with their two cents about "the Boss". Now mind you, the boss was nowhere to be found. It was just the opinions and feelings of the employees that were being discussed, by... that's right... the employees themselves. It was basically a time for uninterrupted and unchallenged ranting and complaining. Have you ever been a part of this little clique? I know I have.

Now here's what I want us to think about for a minute. With all that talk going on, with all that complaining, whining and strategizing about how "they" could do it better than the boss, no one in that group ever really took the comments back to the boss. Why? Because they only wanted to "talk" about it amongst themselves. They weren't looking to fix a problem or even bring a problem to the table for fixing. They were simply "letting off a little steam." You know... 'just talking about it.'

And yet, hiding in plain sight among them was the "office snitch." The one that they could never really name, but the one that was almost invisible during the "chats" and became the most trusted employee to, you guessed it, the boss. That person, disguised as just another employee, would stand around sipping their coffee or water, with their co-workers and be taking mental notes of who said what. They would never inject very much into the conversations either. They would just kind of smile and nod at all of the inappropriate things being said. No one would ever have guessed that they were saving all of the information from the conversations to be used at a later date. And why were they doing this????? Because the inflammatory information, the comments of disunity, and the knowledge of who said what about whom gave them the upper hand with the boss.

In all of the years that I have been in the workforce, and no, I am not going to tell you how many it has been, it has never ceased to amaze me that this person, this office snitch, this invisible force of nature that caused many people to lose their jobs, has been employed at the same places I have, waiting in the wings to take the tidbits of chatter to the person who should never have heard it, the boss.

Now, again, I must remind you that I am in no way insinuating that Bigthan and Teresh were just talking and not plotting. But what I do want us to do is look at how "shop talk" and idle chit chat cannot only be used against us, but used for the gain of others at our expense. Although we say "talk is cheap", in cases like this, it is not. It costs somebody a lot, and sometimes, that somebody is even us.

Once again, the Lord has used a passage of scripture to remind me and teach me again, the importance of discernment. I need to be aware of the times that I jump right in to conversations that I should hurry away from. My prayer is that He will continue to nudge me when I need it the most. Like at the water cooler.

Chapter 22

I have looked at this portion of scripture from a couple of different angles now, and I am sure that all of us will agree, discernment is indeed the better part of valor. Knowing when to keep quiet and walk away from the "water coolers" in our lives is one of the best lessons that we can learn (Rom. 12:18). But what about the time when the situation calls for action? What about when you KNOW that there could be serious repercussions if you stay silent? This is the situation that Mordecai finds himself in. Let's take another look at vs. 21-23.

When Mordecai learns of the plot to harm the king, he has two choices. Walk away and pretend he heard nothing or find someone and explain the situation. Now, put yourself in his shoes for just a moment. This is the Persian empire. Persian. Obviously he is not a Persian by birth but is living within their empire by choice. Apparently, he has a loyalty to the empire. But is it to the king????

As we have discussed in earlier writings, there is unrest and anger at the city gate. Scripture doesn't tell us exactly why Teresh and Bigthan are furious with the king. It doesn't need to tell us. The lesson isn't about their anger. The lesson isn't even about their actions. The lesson is about the righteous actions of Mordecai.

Positionally speaking, Mordecai couldn't just walk right into the throne room and have a chat with King Ahasuerus. Although he has a position of good standing now, it would not have been *that* good. Add to that that he is the "new" guy and most likely doesn't have the same circle of friends or influence that Bigthan and Teresh have. These two men were the king's men. Appointed by the king and trusted by the king. But the conversation is overheard, so what is he to do? Seek out the one person in the kingdom that you know will listen. His cousin, Queen Esther.

Because he is a close relative of the queen, he most likely would be given an audience with her anytime that he requested it. Bringing the news to Esther that her husband's life had been threatened would seem to be the most appropriate thing to do, right? But at the same time, it is also a very dangerous thing to do. Remember what I said before about Teresh and Bigthan? They were servants of the king. Trusted servants of the King of Persia. And if there is one thing that we have learned about old King Ahasuerus it is that he is prideful and arrogant. Would he even believe them if they told him?

Mordecai literally takes his life into his own hands by bringing this news to Esther. If word got out that he had brought this message to her, well his life wouldn't be worth very much now would it? He has nothing to gain by telling the truth, yet he has everything to lose. If the king chose NOT to believe him he could be banished from the kingdom at the very least or hung from the gallows for stirring up trouble. The weight of this grave situation is a heavy one folks. And now, he has come to the queen, the new queen and his own cousin mind you, with this story of betrayal. In order to do the right thing, he has stepped out in faith, that the right thing will be done for him.

Here is something else that was brought to my attention, another scenario for our consideration. Suppose that Mordecai made the decision to keep quiet because he was afraid. And then let's suppose that Teresh and Bigthan made good on their threat and had the king killed. Can you just imagine what would happen to Queen Esther? She could have been executed immediately or worse yet, tortured and abused. Mordecai of course would have been put to death too for his role. When I gave this some thought, I once again saw the working hand of God. He was in control the whole time. Pretty amazing for both Mordecai and Esther wouldn't you say? God uses their disobedience of being in Shushan in the first place, and displays His faithfulness for His people.

There are many times in our lives when fear controls what we do as well as what we don't do. Doing the right thing is not always easy. The right thing can cause us to have a true and very real fear for the outcome. But... the right thing still and always will be the right thing. James 4:17 says, "Therefore, to him who knows to do good and does not do it, to him it is sin."

When Esther hears Mordecai out, she then takes the message to Ahasuerus. "In Mordecai's name." Wow......no "little birdie told me" here folks. She tells the king upfront where the information came from. I would imagine that it lent credibility to the story, wouldn't you? After all, the bearer of the news, Mordecai, had absolutely nothing to gain here. He would have had no reason to make up a story about Teresh and Bigthan. The only thing that was on the table for him was the knowledge that he had done a good and right thing.

But even beyond that, the king did the right thing too. Look at verse 23 again, please. An inquiry was made and the matter was confirmed. King Ahasuerus actually did the right thing here. He didn't just take Mordecai's word for it where this horrific bit of gossip was concerned. He had it checked out to make certain that it was true. And this is where it caused me to stop and think about myself.

How many times have I been guilty of NOT checking something out before I repeat it???? Have you ever done that? Once again the Lord's words convicted me of the times in my life when I had been guilty of this very thing. And then, when it was too late, the "rumor" is found to be just that... a rumor. Oh, if I could turn back the hands of time and put a zipper across my mouth I would. But, since I can't go back in time, I can choose to go forward and learn from my mistakes and not repeat them. And that my friends, is what I choose to do.

Mordecai's warning saves the king. Esther gains favor with the king for telling him the truth. Bigthan and Teresh are hung on the gallows. And another day comes to an end in Shushan. But not before the story is logged into the Book of the Chronicles to be read again at a later time.

Chapter 23

Wow, we finally made it to chapter 3!! I must tell you that once again, just like in our study of Ruth, I have learned more about myself than I really wanted to. I identified with this lesson and it wasn't pleasant for me either. The water cooler is now off limits to me!!

Right off the bat in verse 1, please note that it says "After these things." Remember, that means that a period of time has elapsed. It is not the next day. It is not even the next week. As a matter of fact, according to the chapter timelines in my study Bible, this is written between the seventh and twelfth years of King Ahasuerus' reign. This would mean that Esther has now been the Queen for about 4 years. With there being such a large gap in the writing, it may be safe to assume that things have been relatively quiet in the kingdom. But that, my friends is about to change.

As time has advanced, it seems so has the career of a new member to our story. Let me introduce you to Haman. We learn in this first verse that he is the son of Hammedatha, the Agagite. Living at this time in the Persian Empire, there would have been several different "families." Different cultures, different heritages, different blood lines of peoples lived throughout this mighty kingdom. Just as the writer told us about Mordecai and Esther's family tree, he does the same with Haman. In order to get a full picture of Haman, we must take a moment to understand from whence he came.

Travel back in time with me to Egypt, oh let's say about 1000 years earlier, ca.1445 B.C., and glance at the book of Exodus. I won't take the time to recount all of the happenings that brought the

Israelites to Egypt, nor am I going try and explain the book of Exodus, well not at this time anyway. Maybe later we will study this book??? Anyway, what I want us to look at is in chapter 17:8-16. Amalek brought his army to do battle with the Israelites as they camped in Rephidim. Now who is Amalek, you may be asking right about now? Well, he is the grandson of Esau. Remember Esau? He is the strong red-haired, first born of Rebekah, Isaac's wife. Perhaps you remember his twin brother Jacob? Oh if I only had the time to go into more detail I would. But alas, I am supposed to be writing about Haman, right? So let's get back to him.

As I said previously, Haman's people are descendants of the Amalakites (which the Lord had cursed and despised for their attack on Israel). In 1Sam.15:2-3, King Saul was commanded to kill all of the Amalekites, but he didn't. He let their king, Agag, live. Bad decision on his part too. It is Samuel that steps up to the plate and does the Lord's will and kills Agag (1Sam.15:32,33). Even though the events of Esther happen about 550 years after the death of Agag, well, suffice it say that there is still an anger that burns in the heart of Haman toward the people that killed his king. Even though, Haman was born hundreds of years later, he carried this feeling deep within him. Once again, it is the emotions of our human frailty that rule our outward actions.

Have you ever carried a grudge around? You know... the old chip on your shoulder thing? Someone says something or does something to you and from that moment on you "feel" differently about them. Deep within, you wish them ill. Behind their back you think of ways to "pay them back" for the hurt they caused you. Oh, you may have to continue to work with them, or live around them, but deep within you, you plot and scheme to pay them back. Haman is a perfect example of this kind of behavior. He is carrying around a grudge against the Jewish people. He has a deep-seeded hatred for not just a person, but an entire race of people. A grudge so deep and powerful, that it makes the old Hatfield and McCoy feud seem like child's play. One that we might never had known about had it not been for his career advancement.

You see, for whatever reason, King Ahasuerus has appointed Haman to oversee all of the princes that serve with him. Some writers equate that to what we would we call a Prime Minister. He was second in command of the great Persian Empire. And as most times happens with people in a great seat of authority, it goes to his head. All of the sudden a man that had not even been mentioned before becomes the "boss." If they would have had water coolers back then well... I can only imagine the chit chat that went on. Why? Because as so often happens when positions of responsibility change, people change. And not always for the better either.

"And all of the king's servants who were within the king's gate bowed and paid homage to Haman, for so the king had commanded concerning him." All? Everyone?

Chapter 24

As it happens quite frequently in my studies, I have once again found myself wondering and then wandering around to get a full picture of what is going on in this section of scripture in chapter 3. And, as often times happens, I am searching to understand the phraseology used here. Wow, phraseology... that's a pretty cool word, and it means "choice of words." I believe that the words used here in verse 2 give us a "choice view" into the heart and soul of the matter.

As Haman has been elevated to a new position of respect in his career, it seems that his ego followed along with him. Overseeing the princes of the provinces would indeed be a position of authority and one that would command respect. To me, it is kind of like when a high ranking military man passes by the troops. They salute him out of respect. But, here, at the gate, these are servants of the king, judges for the daily affairs of the empire so why are they supposed to "bow and pay homage?" You know me, I tend to wonder about these kind of things. It is not because Haman has done anything to *deserve* their respect, it is because the position he *now* has deserves the respect. Big difference.

There have been many times in my working career when someone has been promoted to a new position of authority. I might have never really cared for them as a working partner, but when they were promoted, I was forced to respect their new position. Have you ever had to do that? Not always easy either. But be that as it may, we are expected and commanded to respect those in authority. So we bite our tongues, so to speak, and make the most out of the situation.

But here, within theses verses, something else is commanded of the underlings of Haman, something that unless you comprehend the word and the action, you may miss out on the seriousness of the command and the offense of disobedience. Pay "homage" is the word that the NKJV uses. This is something much more legalistic in nature. In this definition it is the acceptance and acknowledgment that you are under the lordship of this person and that they basically own you and your possessions. The term is also described as paying a "feudal fee" to the lord, in this case Haman. Hmmm. If we used that interpretation of the word, not only did this new role bring Haman respect, it seems that it also put money in his pocket. Haman had not only been raised up in his career, but he had also been raised up to a whole new social and economic level. Much in the same way that the servants paid taxes to the king, they would now also pay a fee to Haman for his protection. Why would they need to pay for his protection when they already had the king's protection? This section has caused me to want to study this "feudal law" issue more deeply.

But, in the KJ Version, the word used to translate the Hebrew word *shachah* is 'reverenced.' Now that is different in that there is a more personal response evoked. The word *reverence* means to be in awe of someone or something. It implies that the person showing the reverence has feelings toward or for the person or thing that they are revering. It is obvious to me, that Mordecai doesn't respect or admire Haman. But why? What is there within their relationship that would cause Mordecai to so blatantly show such a degree of disrespect to the positional office that Haman holds?

Then I began to wonder about Mordecai not bowing down to Haman. Have you thought about that? Living within this culture, it would have been proper for the servants of the empire to bow out of respect when the king came by, much like we see today when the leaders of a country address their people. It is a respect thing, for the "role" of the person, not necessarily for the person himself. There are many, many countries today, where the leaders are not respected by their subjects, so the action of bowing before them is well, just that, an ordered action. The law requires them to "bow" and so they do. But when the leader is NOT there, in their presence, how they think of him, well, it is a whole other thing. No one can make another person think a certain way. Your thoughts are your own. But, a person in authority can *make* a person act a certain way in their presence, right? The Persian Empire demanded that subjects would bow before the king but here, they are now required to bow before another political leader. It seems to me that since the king himself had to order that they bow, maybe they had never been required to do that before.

And it is here, in this verse, that Mordecai puts a stake in the ground. He draws a line in the sand and says, "I just can't do that." Have you ever had to draw a line in the sand when you have been asked, or commanded to do something that you just couldn't do? As Christians living and working in a very non-Christian world, I think a good majority of us face our own "line in the sand" times a lot. There are just certain things in my daily life that I just can't be a part of any longer. Ways of life, business ethics, the dog eat dog mentality of the workplace, the *every man for himself* attitude, that well, just leave me shaking inside. Maybe, this was Mordecai's moment when he realized that although he made a choice to live within this empire, he didn't have to live *like* this empire.

It is not easy to live by your convictions. It certainly isn't a smart thing to do in Mordecai's case because the repercussions can be disastrous. But as in all situations, good or bad, we have to make a choice. And the choice for Mordecai was that he would not bow or pay homage to Haman. Although he may not have been living the ultimate lifestyle of a Jewish man he still chose to follow the law of the Lord from Deut.6:4. He would bow to no man, nor any idol. He would bow and show reverence to the one true God, his God. The God of his people. The same wonderful and gracious God that we serve as well. How then shall we live?

Chapter 25

As I read and then re-read this section of the study, there were a couple of thoughts that I wanted to share with you before we move on. There are, of course, some things that we may never be 100% sure of as to the what, where and how of things. But one thing we can see, and see very clearly, is the working of the sovereign Lord God as He guides and directs the entire situation.

As I went through this study with my email Bible study friends, I received an interesting message from our friends, Kelly and Gary (thanks ya'll) who also had felt the urge to wander through the scriptures and get a better picture of Haman and Mordecai. You see, if you don't really take the time to get to know *who* they are, you will not get a good picture of *how* they are. I know, I know, we went over this in the previous lessons, but well... you know me, I can't just go to sleep at night when I haven't figured things out. So, I did a bit more research on old Mr. Haman and I want to share it with you. So go on... get a fresh cup of coffee and we'll sit a spell and see what some of the other Bible scholars have to say about him.

As you know in chapter 3:1, it says that Haman is the son of Hammedatha the Agagite. Remember we talked about the Amalekites. The Lord had instructed King Saul to completely kill the Amalekites because they had attacked His people. Now, remember, Saul didn't do as he was told to do. He let the king live and kept the best of the flocks and herds too. It was Samuel at a later date that actually puts the sword to King Agag. So, here is where the problem lies. If the Amalekites were all killed, and the word all usually means

ALL, how would it be possible that Haman is a descendant? I must admit I got to wondering about that. Did you?

Well, let me offer a very plausible reason how this could have happened. The peoples and tribes that lived in the Old Testament times were nomadic. They moved from place to place all the time. It would not have been unusual at all that some of the family members of the Amalekites lived hundreds of miles away. My own family lives in different parts of the United States, but they are still my blood relatives. Just because we don't live in the same village, so to speak, doesn't make us any less family. As a matter of fact, sometimes families actually *enjoy* living miles apart !!! You know what they say... absence makes the heart grow fonder.

When the Amalekites attacked the Israelites God ordered them destroyed. The "all" could be referring to those of that present tribe of Amalekites. It would have been impossible for those "wandering" Amalekites to have been included in this order from the Lord since the Israelites wouldn't have even known where to look for them. There is also scripture that declares God's wrath on the rest of the Amalekites, but that is another study within itself. My point is this, God's order was carried out on the attacking Amalekites and as for the rest of them, well, their punishment would be doled out to them in God's perfect timing.

Another possible reason that he is called an Agagite would be territorial. Some commentary writers believe that it has to do with the area from which he may have been born or that his family lived. Much like folks that live or come from Boston are called Bostonians. My neighbors here in Fort Worth, you guessed it, are called Fort Worthians. Even though we are not all related by blood, we are related by the area that we choose to live in. Think about this, even when we move far away from our original birthplace, we still call that home. I know that even after several years of living in Texas, I still call California home sometimes.

Now, here is another theory that I read on the term "Agagite". It seems that this term is used to describe a person that is an anti-Semite, or as the scripture says, a hater of the Jews. The term is described as almost a racial slur. When a group or individual is viewed as a "Jew hater" they are called an Agagite in reference to King Agag. In this respect, if Haman is deemed an Agagite, it is not due to his family heritage, it is due to his own personal attitude towards God's people.

Each of these ideas are acceptable to me. Personally, I always had leaned towards the idea that the original family might have been separated by miles and so the DNA lived on. Why? I think because I have tried to reason with myself why Haman was so hateful towards the Jews. If he was a family member of this cursed bloodline that would make sense to me. But on the other hand, I see Haman as a fiercely hateful and spitefully arrogant individual who could very possibly be no blood relation to the Amalekites at all. He is called an Agagite because, well, he hates the entire Jewish race, as we will see in the next few verses. And trust me when I say he is not the first person in history to feel this way about God's people nor will he be the last. We don't have to search very far in our history books to come up with others, even those from our own generation, who have sought to destroy the Israelites. Just listen to the news of the day. It is filled with stories of events in our own time of the Jews still being sought after to be annihilated. Their neighbors are firing rockets into their cities today with this very quest in their hearts to destroy God's people.

The bottom line for me is this, I believe that the word of God is 100% true and perfect. It there is a bit of it that I don't fully understand He will, in His good time, make it clear to me. And He will make it clear to you too. I may never know exactly what verse 3:1 really means, whether Haman is a descendant of the Agagites by blood or by personality, in the big picture it really doesn't matter. Scripture tells me he is what he is and so, I take the Lord's word as the final authority. This will be one of the many questions I have on my "Now that I am here in heaven Lord can you straighten me out on this" list. All in good time, friends. All in the Lord's good and *perfect* time.

Oh, but now you are asking yourself about Mordecai aren't you? Should we wonder about him and his attitude too and do a bit more wandering? Let's look at what God's word has to say.

Chapter 26

Since we spent some time looking into the personality of Haman, I thought it only fair that we also take a look at Mordecai. Each man plays an integral role in this portion of our study. Each man carves a name for himself in the history books. Each man is an instrument of the kingdom he serves. Their kingdoms of choice are very different indeed. Let's take a look.

Until this point in the study, I have viewed Mordecai as a man who is making the best of the situation by making choices that are living outside of what the Lord requested. Suffice it to say, that if Mordecai and Esther were living in Jerusalem, this written part of history wouldn't be here. But, they are here, living, working, and now in direct service to the king. So why then, does Mordecai take it upon himself to bring havoc to the rest of Jews by showing disrespect to Haman? Why now?

Have you ever done a good deed for someone and not received so much as a polite "thank you" in return? Or how about a time when you went out on a limb to assist someone and when they had an opportunity to give you a "tip of the hat" they didn't even so much as put their hand on the brim of the hat? A kind word of thanks or a small gesture of appreciation goes a very long way. But... when we are overlooked, when our good deed or kindness is passed by without as much as a nod of the head, well that's almost... infuriating!!!

Case in point, and of course, I can only use myself as an example here, unless some of you fine folks want to share your trials and tribulations with me (hint, hint). I can think back on many occasions when I have done an act of kindness for someone else and they out the the selfishness of their own heart have not bothered to show me the sincere appreciation that I KNOW I deserve !!! Ouch, ouch, ouch, Mrs. Downer. Did I really just say that? Did I really just admit to all of you that I demand in my mind some over the top word of praise from others when I feel like they should give it???? Do I hear any of you in the background saying "Been there, done that???" There is nothing quite so awful, as when you think that you should get something and no one is delivering it to you.

Praise, respect and acknowledgement are things that all of us crave. And what happens when we don't receive the accolades or rewards that we feel we should get? Usually, we hold a grudge. A big ol' chip on our shoulder that weighs us down. We carry it around with us and it effects everything we do from that point on. At first I thought to myself, "Why are you showing me this, Lord? Certainly You are not trying to reveal something like this to me about... well... ME, are you?"

Remember back a few verses ago when Mordecai brings word to Esther about the plot to kill the king? And remember how thankful and grateful King Ahasuerus was to Mordecai? Remember how the mighty king brought Mordecai out in front of all of his other servants and praised him for his good deed? What? You don't remember the king thanking Mordecai? Well, guess what. Your memory hasn't failed, because the king doesn't acknowledge Mordecai publicly at all. As a matter of fact, the king, Mordecai's cousin's husband says nothing at all to him. Nada. Zippo. Zilch.

I have read a couple of different commentaries that suggest that this situation may have perturbed Mordecai just a smidge. After all, the Persian kings were known for their generosity in situations like this. It would have nothing at all for this very wealthy king to have blessed Mordecai with a mighty fortune for this good deed or at the very least, to have raised him up within the kingdom to a position of trust and authority. Kind of like his "right hand man." That would have been a great idea. But instead of Mordecai getting the recognition that he so deserves, it is his co-worker Haman who gets it. And for what? What did he do that was so great?????

Here is where some say that Mordecai might have started to carry around a bit of a chip on his shoulders towards Haman. Now I know, scripture tells us that Haman was a hater of the Jews, but I must point out, we are not told that until *after* Mordecai has disrespected him. And I remind you again, that bowing down to those in authority was not something new to Mordecai. He probably did it on countless occasions because that was the law of the empire that he lived in. It had nothing to do with the person as much as it had to do with the position. So why not just bow and go about his business?

How often are we put in this kind of position where we have to show respect to authority that we deem to be unworthy? Could Mordecai have had a bad feeling like we have had? In his heart did he want so badly what the other person got, that he was blinded by anything else? Maybe, just maybe, Mordecai was a tad bit more like us than he should have been.

I might not like it when others receive what I think I so richly deserve. I might secretly and quietly hold a grudge against them and for what? When all is said and done, will anyone really remember who got what for doing what for whom? I need to give it up folks. I need to bury the hatchet, get my head out of the sand and realize that life isn't always fair. Why? Because we live in a sinful fallen world. But I have hope. For me. For you. And for anyone ready to take it. We serve a risen Savior and he will dole out to us ALL and more of the blessings that are most important. HIS.

Chapter 27

Sometimes when I read back over our study, I am amazed and shocked that I reveal the things about myself to you. Who knew? I go through life most days thinking that I am a pretty "nice" person until I realize that deep within me, just like some of the people in our story, my motives for doing the things I do (or don't do for that matter) are not of the purest intent. I want what I want when I want it, and by gum, I want people to give it to me. Let's see how old Mr. Haman responds to wanting what he wants.

As we rejoin our little group in Esther 3:3, we see that the other servants that are working the gate area focus their attention on Mordecai. Oh not because of what Mordecai is doing, but because of what Mordecai *isn't* doing. Bowing down and paying homage to Haman. I can almost hear them say something like this: "Hey Mordie, *wassupp* bro??? Why are you doing the *diss* dance for Haman?" Can't you just *feel* the love here???

What strikes me in this verse is the genuine concern these fellow servants had for Mordecai and the trouble that he might get himself into for showing such a lack of respect to Haman. NOT!!! Notice that they didn't pull him aside and express their concern for his well being. They wanted to know one thing and one thing only. How come *they* had to bow if Mordecai didn't. How come the rules didn't apply to Mordecai? Notice that it doesn't take the click and clack brothers very long to go sing the blues to Haman either. It seems like these two fellow co-workers couldn't wait to go and "click their tongues and clack their jaws" in order to make certain that Mordecai is on the hot seat.

Have you ever worked with people like that? They spin their wheels and spend their time going around and around trying to justify why so and so should or shouldn't be doing this or that. It is not because they have this deep respect for the order-giver either. It is because if they have to do it, bowing down in this case, then so should everyone else. It is only fair right? Well folks I gotta say, if I have learned anything in my years on this planet, it is that the word "fair" is not written on my birth certificate. Life isn't always fair. There are times when we look around and look for justice and it is nowhere to be found. As long as life is not treating us so fairly, well why not make sure everyone gets treated the same way. Ugh, ugh and double ugh!!

I find it hard to believe that these two guys wouldn't have known enough about Haman to know that any show of disrespect was going to be addressed. Remember, it has been at least a few years since the royal palace added Mordecai as a gate servant. He has most likely known these gentlemen for quite some time. That would make sense to me. How about you? Why then, if they knew him, didn't they kind of reach out to him and well, protect him instead of turning him in to face Haman's wrath? Come on now. Think about this. Old Haman was so busy strutting his stuff, he didn't even notice that Mordecai wasn't bowing. These guys had to *tell* him. Pretty self-absorbed, if you ask me.

You know, I was thinking that just maybe, Mordecai would have been forgiven this grievous sin by Haman since Jewish culture required him not to bow to a *man*. It is not like Mordecai is the only Jew living in the empire. And it is not like Haman would not have known that about the Jewish people. This offense could have very simply and very humbly have been overlooked. But as we find out in the next verses, it is not. As a matter of fact, Haman becomes filled with wrath and plans to put an end to Mordecai's selfish behavior.

Have you ever been in a situation where you wanted someone to act a certain way and you just couldn't stand it that they didn't? It was personal. Your heart burned with anger and you just couldn't stand that they were disrespecting you. It happens in the workplace all the time. This situation is no different in its beginning stages than what a lot of us face each day. Why? Because we are sinful humans that want what we want when we want it and in the way that we want it. The only difference in our behavior is in the outcome.

The "Tattler Twins" have set the stage. Haman is now in a snit about Mordecai. Will he ask him to step into his office for a chat or will he just hand out punishment for his actions? In this case, as you will see, actions will speak louder than words.

.

Chapter 28

"*The desire of the righteous is only for good, but the expectation of the wicked is wrath*," Proverbs 11:23. Talk about a perfect verse to describe what is happening in Shushan right now.

One of the things that we discussed previously was the family tree of Haman. Was he an Agagite by birth lineage or was he just called one because of his utter detest of the Jews. Well, in looking at verses 5-9, we catch a glimpse of how deeply his hatred runs.

Once Haman is aware of the infraction and the friction caused by Mordecai's transgression, he had several choices he could make. He could address Mordecai privately and discuss the situation, turn his cheek to the offense and allow Mordecai the quiet "right" to this disobedience of the new Persian law, or he could force his hand and insist that Mordecai obey the law and bow down to him and pay homage. But wait. There seems to be yet another choice here, one that most of us would never dream of. Execution.

Just like any of the other Persian laws, this too could hold the punishment of death. Haman could have immediately turned to his subordinates and demanded that Mordecai be executed for his show of disrespect. Once Haman learned who Mordecai's people were he would set out to kill them all. My NKJV uses the word "disdain" to describe how Haman feels. Disdain means to have a "feeling of contempt for what is beneath one." Now there's a word that paints a picture.

Haman not only held a position that placed him in authority above others, but his ego rose to a level that he now looked down his nose at those beneath him. Have you ever had to deal with someone who thought themselves so high and mighty that they would break their neck if they tripped over themselves? Their head was so high in the clouds that the lack of oxygen made them, well, dizzy. They seem to be coming from an entirely different world and reality. They are so self-absorbed and so inwardly focused that they couldn't see the forest through the trees. Everything was about them and them only. And once more, I am forced to wonder if I have ever acted this way. Have you? So proud. So righteous. So... ugh.

To say that old Haman had a grudge against the actions of Mordecai is mild compared to what he is feeling towards the whole of the Jewish nation of people. If Haman had no ties of any kind to the past history between the Jews and the Amalakites, how is it that all of sudden he wants to destroy anyone that holds to the Jewish religion? There just has to be a deeper reason for his reaction to Mordecai and the action he then chooses. Think about it for a minute. The score he needed to settle was between him and Mordecai. How on earth does that translate into his quest to set out to completely wipe out the Jews? Persecution is nothing new to the Jews. You can read throughout history how God's people have been treated. Sought after. Chased. Tortured and killed. Why? Because they were God's chosen people. I am afraid that this situation is just one of many from the past with more to follow in the future. Regardless of when you are reading this, I challenge you look at what is happening around Israel right now and I am sure that you will see examples of this persecution.

Haman becomes so full of wrath and so filled with rage that he seizes this opportunity to develop a plan so evil that it should make you shiver. I can almost see him pacing back and forth and back and forth rubbing his hands together plotting out his plan of destruction. But how can he pull this off? He is one man aiming to destroy a whole population of people scattered throughout 4.7 million square miles of land folks. Oh, Haman might be the Prime Minister of the empire but he is certainly not Superman. He needs a plan and he needs help. And he needs lots of help.

Chapter 29

We see that Mordecai has taken a stand against the wishes of the king, and refused to bow down and pay homage to Haman. Now Haman, being the type of man that he is, is not going to stand by quietly and let Mordecai just stand by. Instead of taking the time to go to Mordecai and talk about the situation and try to come to a reasonable compromise, Haman does what he does best and plots a plan to take action against Mordecai's insubordination. And friends, quite a plan it is.

What better way to make one solitary man obey your command for respect than to wipe out an entire culture of people. What???? This is the section of scripture where I have indeed looked at the relationship between Mordecai and Haman and just felt secure that there was more to their past than maybe is written within the verses. Looking back at their past has led me to believe that the ill-will that Haman feels goes deeper than just this one instance. Haman has a deeply buried burden of hatred towards the Jews and he uses this occasion to bring it to the forefront dealing with Mordecai.

Once again, I ask the question about holding a grudge. Have you ever carried around a grudge towards someone? The old chip on your shoulder? In your mind you play and replay the wrong that has been done to you and search out a way to get even? And while we are talking about that, have you ever noticed that the grudge you carry grows and grows and GROWS until it manifests itself into a HUGE situation???? Why is that? Why is it that our minds seem to focus on this thing over and over again? It festers like an open wound until its infection almost takes us over.

I have found an answer for myself concerning this and would like to share it with you. Turn with me to the book of Philippians for a moment. In this letter Paul is writing to a group of believers in the church. After Christ. Most people think the focus of this letter is joy, but as our church group studied it these last few weeks we came to understand that it pertains more to unity. The unity of the believers is Paul's call to arms. He wants them to think alike and act accordingly with what they know of Christ. Believe it or not, even Christians back then fussed at one another.

Now turn to Philippians 4:8-9. Read very carefully the things that Paul tells us to think on. Things that are *true*. Things that are *noble*. Things that are *just*, *pure* and *lovely*. Then he adds things of *good report*, things with *virtue* and last but not least, things that are **praiseworthy**!! How often I have fallen victim in my mind of things that are the exact *opposite* of this list!!! I allow myself to dwell on past hurts and heartaches. Yes, that's right, I said, I <u>allow</u> myself to dwell there. It is like giving myself permission to hold these painfully ugly situations up to be inspected and judged over and over again. Please tell me that I am not alone here. I believe this is a good example of what we call our own "stinking thinking!!"

Look closely at the end of verse 9. "And the God of peace will be with you. This is a wonderful promise folks. But one that we can only get IF we make a choice to think and act in the way that Paul describes here in these verses. We need to work diligently each day to train ourselves to replace the thoughts that bring us anger or sorrow with thoughts that will lift our spirits and fill us with joy!!! It is a battlefield in our minds and even outside of our minds. We need to be on the ready to remove, replace and replenish ourselves with the wonderful thoughts of Christ.

As we can see from our verses in Esther, Haman was consumed with his own "stinking thinking." It drove him to the decisions that he made, not just toward Mordecai but, to the entire Jewish race that lived within the Persian Empire.

Every Jewish man, woman and child was to be sought after and killed according to Haman's plan. But the how and when are yet to be decided. Let's find out who Haman seeks to help him formulate his plan shall we?

Chapter 30

Let's get back to our text in Esther. Join me in chapter 3 verse 7. It is interesting that the writer takes the time to tell us not only the month that this is written in, Nissan, but he also adds that it is now the twelfth year of King Ahasuerus' reign. Right there, that tells us that this event, this moment in time, is being accurately recorded for future reference. It is almost as though the writer is aware of the importance of keeping history correctly.

"They cast Pur (that is the lot)." This is one of those hard concepts for me to really get a handle on. Casting lots is mentioned in the Old Testament about 70 times. In some of the writings in the book of Joshua it refers to the land being divided amongst the Israelites. Joshua cast lots before the Lord to determine what parcel of land each family would receive. This was a method that was used when seeking a plan from God. The lot that was cast (similar to our own tradition of rolling dice or drawing straws) was done by man but the result was chosen by God. The participants trusted that God was making this unspoken decision for them.

It is interesting to note that Haman, a pagan, uses this method. The only difference here of course, is that he does not seek Gods divine answer. In verse 7 it says "they." This is referring to his court of advisors. In other words, his astrologers. Similar to the Magi that followed the star to see Jesus, these men, as well as others in the empire including Ahasuerus, followed the Zoroastrian religion. In some of my reading and study of this religion, I find that it is kind of similar in thought to a sort of "works" based reward system. Your good thoughts and deeds are rewarded with eternity. But what is there in eternity for you if there is no Jesus?

Let's get back to Haman and his friends. In all of my wondering and then wandering through the Bible I could not get a firm description of exactly "how" the lots were cast. Whether it be by a type of stick (like a piece of straw), cubes (similar to our dice) or a type of flipping of a two faced coin, I am not sure. And I am not even sure if they drew a calendar of the months to coincide with the lots. But I do know this, through the process of casting lots it was determined that they would attack and completely wipe out all of the Jews living within the Persian Empire "on the thirteenth day of the twelfth month, which is Adar" (vs.13). Pretty precise, isn't it? All of the Jews to be annihilated in ONE day.

Now, if you take a moment and do the math here, there is almost a year from the time the date is decided until the attack will actually take place. This should give Haman and the army of Persia plenty of time to get ready. As we learned in an earlier part of our study, the empire has 4.7 million square miles, which makes it larger than the total area of the continental United States. The Jews could be living anywhere within those miles. Pretty daunting when you think about an army actually setting itself up to go out and seek these people out and kill them.

Once Haman had consulted with his astrologer friends he still had one more hurdle to get over before putting this plan into motion. He needed the permission of the king. Even though Haman held the office of second in command, he could do nothing that would affect the empire to this degree without the permission and blessing of the king. Now remember, King Ahasuerus has already depleted his treasuries with the last attempt at war. Remember Greece? That didn't go well for him at all, his treasuries felt the full force of money lost as well as his own personal humiliation of a battle lost.

So, good old Haman must come up with yet another plan in hopes of getting the king to agree to let him do this. Can't you almost see the wheels turning in his head? Pacing back and forth with his astrologers, rubbing his hands together thinking, thinking, thinking!

Chapter 31

Let's pick up in Esther 3:8. Haman wastes no time here with chit-chat. He gets right to the point. Right down to the nitty-gritty of why he has sought an audience with the king. "There are a certain people scattered and dispersed among the people in the provinces of your kingdom." Let's stop here for a moment and look a bit deeper at the stage that Haman is setting.

Haman paints a picture for the king that this "*certain people*" are somehow bad for the kingdom. Just by starting the sentence off this way, the assumption can be made that "*they*" are somehow different from the Persians. The inference is there. You can almost hear the coyness in his voice as he brings this bit of news to his king. Think about it a minute. King Ahasuerus probably thinks that there is trouble amiss with these people, why else would Haman, his second in command, be bringing him this news if there was nothing wrong?

Well. if King Ahasuerus makes that assumption, he is indeed wrong. There is nothing amiss within his kingdom. At least not with the group of people that Haman is referring to here. But, Haman goes on to explain that "their laws are different than all other people's laws and furthermore, they do not keep the king's laws". Whoa Nelly. Now that is a big deal!!! There would be no way that King Ahasuerus would just sit back on his mighty throne and allow his subjects to be insubordinate to him or his kingdom's laws. His pride would never allow it. And if there is one thing that we know for certain here it is that the king is a very proud man. Remember what happened to Vashti?

But within these verses, Haman never says just "who" these "other people" are, and you will notice that the mighty king never bothers to ask. Verse 8 finishes with Haman telling the king that it "is not fitting for them to remain." Haman, ever the coy master of manipulation, plays right into the king's prideful hand. Haman is telling the king, that to allow these people to stay within the kingdom will put a blemish on him. He plays the king like a fiddle.

And then Haman smoothly adds, "if it pleases the king, let a decree be written that they be destroyed and I will pay ten thousand talents of silver into the hands of those that do the work, to bring to the king's treasuries." *Cha-ching, cha-ching.* When you look at the first few words you might think that Haman is trying to do right by his king and the kingdom. "If it pleases the king." This was a phrase used to let the king know that the decision was totally his to make, but that he (Haman) had the best interests of the king at heart. Pretty slick way to word it. Haman is totally manipulating Ahasuerus with his smooth words to get him (the king) to do exactly want he (Haman) wants.

Have you ever known a smooth talker? We used to have a saying that went, "he could sell ice to an Eskimo." Door to door salesmen or the evening telemarketer that convinces you to subscribe to a paper that you will never read or buy an appliance that will gather dust on your countertop. I am sure that most of us have come in contact with a smooth talker in our day. Sly manipulation by them gets you to do exactly what they want you to and the whole time YOU are feeling like you are in control of the matter. This is what Haman is doing. He convinces the king of a need, in this case to rid the kingdom of these people, then he smoothly offers to take care of the matter, in an attempt to make the king believe that he is looking out for the kingdoms best interest.

Now here is another tid-bit for you. Ten thousand talents of silver is equal to about 300 tons. T O N S!!! I just have to ask... where in the world would Haman keep 300 tons of *anything*??? And, just so you can get the proper perspective of this offer, the kingdom's annual revenue is recorded to be approximately fifteen thousand talents of silver. This offer is 2/3's of the entire kingdom's income for a year. Where in the world would Haman get that kind of money?

And without batting an eye, the king hands over his signet ring to Haman, giving him full authority to write the decree and deliver the decree. It's as if the king just waves his hand in the air while murmuring "yadda, yadda, yadda". Open your hand up for just a moment. Imagine the king's signet ring being placed in your hand. You and you alone, now have the power of the king to make any decision in the entire kingdom. Once that ring was given to Haman, he had the king's full authority to handle this matter, or any matter, in the way that he saw fit.

Here we see yet another side of King Ahasuerus. Uninterested and uninvolved. Some might argue that he trusted Haman to make a good decision concerning these people, as he says at the end of verse 10. But really, I look back at his other encounters with his subjects and see a man in a high position of authority that consistently turns to others to either advise him of what he should do, or just blindly does their bidding without any real input of his own. Once again, I am reminded of his dealings with Vashti. By listening to and then reacting to the ramblings of someone else, Memucan, in the case of Vashti, King Ahasuerus worsened the entire situation by the way he dealt with her. Once again, he shows his true colors and allows someone else to manipulate him into an act that will certainly affect his kingdom in a very negative way. He is not a very good leader.

Once the decree is written and sent by courier to the 127 provinces, there is no going back. There is no, "Oops, I changed my mind." This is not a kingdom where there are second chances, folks. Once his signet ring is used for this decree, it is law *forever*. Not only will this decree to kill all of the Jews, young and old, men and women, affect those within the kingdom, but it also affect some living in the king's own palace as well. One very special someone has just been issued a death warrant.

"...the city of Shushan was perplexed". Do you think maybe they knew something that Ahasuerus didn't?

Chapter 32

The smooth talking Haman has spun his web of deceit and convinced the king that the group of people in the kingdom must be dealt with. Once the king gives his permission, Haman then sits with the scribes to write out the decree. As we know from previous lessons on "scribes" they are similar to legal assistants. Their job is to not only possess intricate knowledge of the laws of the land, but they must also be able translate the laws into all of the foreign languages of the empire too. Not only are they tasked with writing this new decree but they must write it in each of the different languages of the peoples within the kingdom. Not some small task when you think about it.

Verse 12 tells us they wrote the decree according to "all that Haman commanded." Interesting. Notice it doesn't say "as the king commanded". Once again, I am in awe that the mighty King of Persia is on the sidelines here. This decree will inevitably change his kingdom for generations to come. Why hasn't it been noted that he even seems to care? I am struck by the fact that Ahasuerus just kind of follows Haman's lead.

Please take just a moment to look at the wording in verses 12 and 13. Notice that the tone of the command has changed a bit? When Haman discussed the situation with the king back in verse 9 he used the word "destroy." But the following verses include the exact wording for the decree as it now reads "to destroy, to kill and to annihilate." And Haman now includes "all the Jews, young and old, little children and women." The words annihilate and destroy can both mean to wipe out of existence. There would be no trace left that the Jews had ever lived. Like many of the other peoples of the world, the Amalekites, the Hittites and others before them, they would simply... disappear.

May I take a minute to point something out to you that caught my attention? If indeed Haman was trying to protect the king's best interests by bringing to his attention that there is this group of people that were "different," why didn't he just suggest to the king that a decree be sent out that ALL of the kingdom's subjects must follow the Persian law or face being removed from the kingdom? I have a really hard time trying to understand that another human being would order the destruction of an entire human race living within its borders. Is Haman's decree against the Jews so different than what we witness today in some countries around the world? Heartbreaking, isn't it?

At the end of verse 15, scripture tells us that "the king and Haman sat down to drink, but the city of Shushan was perplexed." REALLY???? A celebratory round between the two of them? What exactly are they celebrating? I read an article that said that the Jewish population at this time in Persia would have been about 20% of the entire empire. I just can't help but wonder why Ahasuerus would allow a decree to go out to kill them all. These were probably loyal, law abiding citizens and TAXPAYERS!!!! It is obvious to me that the king is oblivious to what goes on within his own kingdom!! Haman's words of deceit have filled Ahasuerus with paranoia and his reaction is to wipe them all out. Amazing.

Chapter 33

As we conclude chapter 3 of the book of Esther, I want to take a moment and throw out to you another scenario for your consideration. Remember I mentioned that King Ahasuerus was paranoid? You may have asked yourselves, why would I think that? Let me explain.

The Persian Kingdom, although it is HUGE in land mass and size of population it is also in a precarious position. Battles were fought all the time for world dominance. When a kingdom won a battle and took over the land and the people there was a fine balance within the kingdom to keep peace. The conquered people were to be acclimated into the new society and change their lifestyle and fit or be put to death. It is not as though they can just simply gather their belongings and move to another town. They belonged to the new regime.

King Ahasuerus needed all of his subjects to be loyal to his kingdom and his reign. But Haman telling him that there was a group in his kingdom that were not loyal, could very possibly have led the king to believe that there could be an uprising within his kingdom. This would be reason enough for him to react and then act in the manner he did. Fear. Fear that he would be overthrown and removed from his throne. Fear that he would die.

King Ahasuerus sure reminds me of a typical 'yes man.' He is very similar to people that I have worked with or have served on committees with, people that agree with anything that the "leader" is saying. Why? Because the leader of the group or job takes a shine to them and shows them more favor. Leaders need and desire to have "yes men" in their corners, those who simply follow along and don't buck the system or their authority. It makes the leader's job much easier. But sometimes, and I think that we will all agree, what goes on behind the back of the leader... well, let's just say that the "yes man" has ulterior motives and usually makes his move at *just* the right time to upstage the leader!! And this is exactly what Haman does to Ahasuerus. Checkmate.

Don't you think that King Ahasuerus is more of a follower than he is a leader? These verses clearly show a man who lets others make the important decisions and then sits back and awaits the outcome. I think that in his dealings with the king, Haman knew this and so he used the knowledge to his own advantage to gain the outcome that he was seeking, total annihilation of the Jews. And again, I say, Checkmate!!

By taking advantage of the king's natural inclination of fear toward a rebellious take over (and remember, it wasn't so long ago that a plot to take the king's life was discovered) and convincing the king that he has the kingdom's best interest at heart, Haman has unceremoniously and yet most certainly, brought his plan of destruction to the forefront of the kings attention. Once there, once the king got wind of any kind of uprising, the plan that Haman put in front of him was accepted.

"But the city of Shushan was perplexed." The word that is used here, perplexed, is the Hebrew word, "*buwk*" and is only used two other times in scripture. In Exodus 14:3, Pharaoh uses it to describe the condition of the Israelites in the wilderness and then also in Joel 1:18, the word paints a picture of the confusion of the animals as they search for food after the devastation of the plague of the locusts. Hungry. Tired. Turning around and around trying to find enough grass to graze on to keep them alive.

This is the same kind of tormented confusion that the inhabitants of the city of Shushan are feeling. Imagine if you will, that the town crier has stood on the steps of the city gate and read this proclamation about the coming annihilation of the Jews. Can't you just almost hear the whispering among them as they turn to each other and say "WHAT???" To be perplexed is to be totally confused to the point of turning around and around in a quest to find a reasonable answer for something. Going from person to person and back and forth trying to get a firm grasp of the situation. And all the while they are probably standing right beside a person whose very life will be extinguished.

The city of Shushan, very much like any other city within the kingdom, is filled with people of origins other than just Persian. In his commentary on Esther, J. Vernon McGee estimates that there were approximately 15 million Jews living in the Persian Empire at this time. 15 MILLION!! It has been estimated that they make up about 20% of the population. *That is 1 in 5.* And now, with a few stokes of a pen and the seal of the signet ring, the lives of these people will be over. Totally wiped out of existence as though they had never even lived there. Some of you may even remember the horror of the Holocaust where over 6 million Jews were killed by Hitler during World War II

Picture again my friends, the utter heartbreak of knowing that someone you knew, someone you did business with, someone who your own children might have played with, has a death sentence placed on them. Wouldn't you be a tad bit perplexed too? Remember, the Jews have been living, working and raising their families in this empire for many years. They have relationships with the other people that abide here as well. Don't think for a minute that all of those gathered to hear this decree didn't turn to each other in horror and sorrow and perplexity. The gravity of this proclamation would have indeed made them turn around and around, seeking out an answer and an understanding as to why this has been decreed.

Perplexed. Bewildered. Filled to overflowing with uncertainty. Trying to make sense of the senseless. Have you ever felt this kind of emotion? Have the trials and heartache that you have experienced brought you to perplexity? I know that there have been many times in my own life where my own trials have brought me there as well.

Isaiah 48:17 says, "Thus says the LORD, your Redeemer, The Holy One of Israel: "I am the LORD your God, Who teaches you to profit, Who leads you by the way you should go."" Sometimes the thing we desperately need and can't see, *trust*, is the thing that we need the most. Our Lord, then and now, will lead us where we need to go. In the times of perplexity, turn to Him and only Him for the guidance that He will offer. Trust God.

Chapter 34

As we begin chapter 4, we see a man tormented and broken by the result of his actions. Mordecai is feeling the full responsibility of the edict that has been sent out to all of the provinces. In a public display, "he tore his clothes and put on sack cloth and ashes and went out into the midst of the city" 4:1.

Here is a man, a public figure, who is now well known at the city gate, so devastated by the retribution of Haman that he lends himself to humiliation and degradation by coming to the kings gate in sackcloth. The wailing of his heart is loud enough for even his cousin the queen to hear, piercing the comfort zone of Esther and causing, even her, distress.

Have you ever been close enough to someone that you could actually *feel* their wails of sorrow? An emotion so deep and penetrating that shivers ran down your arms? The loss that they are experiencing is almost absorbed into your very soul?

I have.

The pain that they are feeling is so *real*, so *near* to the very core or my heart that it is as though I am somehow transported into their "being".

Bryan and I attended the funeral of a very dear friend's teenaged son. In all of my years here on earth, nothing could have prepared me for the total incredible loss that I felt. A sadness so deep within me that I thought that I wouldn't be able to even do the simple act of breathing the first time I saw her. I wanted so desperately to be strong for her, but when I reached out to hug her and whisper words of comfort to her, I found that the words I so wanted to say were lost in the sound of my own anguish for her. Her human emotion, her need to be comforted, was met with the unabashed tears of another mother experiencing her pain as though it was my own. Sometimes there just aren't enough words to say. All we can do is wail.

Mordecai's loud cries are heard within the palace walls and Esther is summoned by her servants. She knows not what has happened yet. The decree to administer death to her countrymen would not have reached her ears yet. We see that in verse 4. She is perplexed as to what could have possibly happened to Mordecai to cause this outburst. As much as she would desire to bring him into the palace to comfort him, she can't. He can't enter the king's gate in sackcloth and ashes. So she quickly gathers clothes for him and sends them to him by her servant Hathach. But soon, Hathach returns with the news that Mordecai will not accept the clothing, which means, she cannot see him face to face.

The Bible references "sackcloth and ashes" many times, starting as far back as the book of Genesis. It was used as a public display of the person's inner despair and distress. The sackcloth was normally made from goat's hair and was worn close to the skin. The discomfort that the wearer experienced added to the emotional feeling of the situation. In other words, the discomfort they felt in their heart was multiplied and kept in the forefront of their thoughts by the discomfort their physical body was feeling.

By covering themselves in ashes the person becomes unclean. According to Hebrew law, if they were unclean they would be separated from their family. This could be a symbol of that the type of separation that the Jews were experiencing. Alone. Lost in their sorrow. Solitary in their own distress. This is how Mordecai might have felt. In his act of obedience to his God, he has brought the wrath of his lord (Haman) upon his innocent countrymen. Can you just imagine the devastation and remorse that he must be feeling?

It is never easy to do the right thing. It is never right to just do the easy thing either. Mordecai knows with every fiber of his being, that his act, his rebellious act against Haman has unleashed the power of a very evil man. There is no one for Mordecai to blame for this. It is his doing and he knows it. And so he grieves his mistake. He dresses in sackcloth and ashes, enters the middle of the crowded city and throws his head back and wails. There are no words. There are only the solemn sobs of a man in mourning.

What will he tell Esther? How can he possibly explain what has happened. And even more important.....what will Esther do?

Chapter 35

Most of us in our societies today have never put on sackcloth and ashes. I must admit that when I first read this section, I thought to myself, this doesn't apply to me Lord, because it is not a "custom" that we do. You see, I kept seeing it as a religious "custom" that only the Jews did. I needed to look a bit deeper to see how the Lord was using this section to teach me something about myself. And maybe you should, too.

The reason that Mordecai presents himself at the king's gate in sackcloth and ashes actually has more meaning to it than just someone desiring to make a public spectacle of themselves in an effort for others to take notice of them and see the sorrow that they are experiencing. Mordecai is placing himself in a position that will bring him humiliation, degradation and possible retribution from those he stands before. Not only is he standing in the midst of the Persian population, but right beside him, right next to where he is weeping, are the other Jews that also have made Shushan their home. Don't think for a minute that those around him are not also crying and shouting in dismay dressed in sackcloth and ashes (vs. 3).

There is no amount of remorse that Mordecai can feel that will change the outcome of his actions. None. The penalty for his error in judgment will now put innocent blood on his hands. Try as I might, as I sit here, I cannot fathom how utterly devastated and destroyed he must be feeling. And responsible. Mordecai and Mordecai alone carries this responsibility. The burden of this sin must be totally overwhelming. And that's when it hit me.

The burden of my own sins. The times when my disobedience to the Lord's will was so apparent and so blatant that it now brings a stirring discomfort to my soul. The choices I made, the path that I chose to follow, the many "me" times, that brought heartache to those around me, are innumerable. My stubbornness. My faithlessness. My unrepentant and unforgiving heart. The many times that I let my family or myself down from the choices I made. The many times I ran *from* God instead of running *to* Him !! Oh, if I only would have had sackcloth and ashes back then.

But do you know what I did have and still have buried deep in my closet? A nice old worn-in comfy pair of sweat pants. You know the kind I am talking about, don't you. They are the ones that hardly have any elastic left around the waist so they allow for plenty of belly room after a big meal that I *know* I shouldn't be eating!! They have been washed so many times that the feel of the cloth against my skin is light and airy almost. Not burdensome. Not cumbersome. As Goldilocks once said "They are just right".

Had sin really become that... comfortable to me???? Did I so readily accept my failures and shortcomings as just a human nature thing? Did I so easily forget that my mistakes, my bad choices left God Himself weeping for me? Or was it more that I really didn't get it? I really didn't understand that the Lord God Almighty really did care about me and for me?

And that my friends is what the Lord showed my in these verses. His undying and totally unwavering love for me. And for YOU!!

I now have a deeper understanding of sackcloth and ashes. The Lord in His mighty wisdom and mercy has put them within my soul. I now *feel* the sin in my life and can no longer live with its discomfort. The sackcloth rubs on my skin and convicts me to change my path. Change my mind. Change my heart.

An outward sign of an inward change. That is what my prayer is, that every day in every way, I can be reminded of the great and unfailing love of the Father. All so that I can strive a little harder to be a little better and that the times when I fall become less and less.

A sinner saved by grace. Perfect plan from a Perfect God!!!

Chapter 36

"Deliver those who are drawn toward death, and hold back those stumbling to the slaughter. If you say 'Surely we did not know this,' does not He who weighs the hearts consider it? He who keeps your soul, does He not know it? And will He not render to each man according to his deeds?" Proverbs 24:11-12.

The verses that we have been looking at in chapter 4:1-5 speak to me loudly and clearly about the sovereignty of God. He knows exactly what is going on here in Shushan, and He knows exactly the who, what, where, and how of the entire situation and its outcome. He will use the evil intent of Haman to bring Mordecai to the position of saving His chosen people. But Mordecai needs help and he has come to the city gate to get it, from none other than the Queen herself.

Once Hathach returned with the new clothing that Esther sent to Mordecai, Queen Esther knew for sure that something was horribly wrong with her cousin. At this point she has not been enlightened to the decree that the king sent out. But Hathach goes out to Mordecai and returns again with not only the spoken words of Mordecai's plea for help but the written words of the death warrant in his hand, for the Queen to read for herself. There is no mistaking at all that Mordecai needs her to fully comprehend the absolute emergency that is at hand.

As Mordecai is explaining to Hathach the graveness of the situation, he tells him to take the written decree to Esther that "he might show it to Esther and explain it to her and that he might command her to go to the king to make supplication to him and plead for her people," verse 8. Now wait a minute here folks. Just exactly

WHAT is Mordecai suggesting here? I have read this verse over and over again and I can't help but notice the "tone" of voice I hear within the written word. "Command???" Is he really suggesting that this eunuch, the queen's servant *suggest* that she do anything???? If I was that servant I would have turned to Mordecai and said "REALLY"???

If there is one thing that is absolutely not tolerated in this kingdom it is insubordination!! We have already seen examples of what happens to those that "rock the boat." The mere suggestion to this servant that he try and tell his queen to do anything would be a mistake and a half. His life could be over within a matter of minutes if she decided that he was being disrespectful. But obviously Mordecai feels secure in the relationship that he has not only with Esther but with the relationship that Esther has with the servant!! There just possibly might be a bond of trust there. As a matter of fact, I think there must be or she would not have sent Hathach out to Mordecai in the first place. Remember, by dressing in the sackcloth and ash, her cousin has identified himself publicly as a Jew. And if he is one... well... it won't take long for others within the palace to find out she is one too.

Now I am not a rocket scientist, folks, and I don't think that I need to be one to understand the pickle that Esther is in. She has lived very comfortably in the palace now for over five years. Her identity is only that of Queen. She is safe within that identity. As commanded by Mordecai many years earlier, she has told no one that she is Jewish. It was a secret well kept. But as they say where I come from, "The cat is out of the bag."

Will Esther respond to the solemn plea of Mordecai or will she close the curtains at her window and pretend she never saw him out there in the street? Can her life within the palace ever be the same?

Chapter 37

As we finish this section of chapter 4, we see that Esther has received the disarming news from Mordecai about the decree to annihilate the Jews. She must be experiencing fear, pain, sorrow and confusion. No one in the citadel or the empire would have seen this coming. They have lived peacefully side by side for many years. Working together. Children playing together. I just cannot imagine the turmoil that everyone must be in.

In thinking back to the previous verses, we must remember that the decree, although it has been sent out, took some time to prepare. Remember when Haman and the astrologers were casting lots for the day of the massacre? There was almost a year to wait. This would not only allow the army of Persia to prepare, but it also gave the Jews time to prepare as well. But wait a minute. Did you realize that since the army could not possibly handle this kind of massacre, it would have been their own neighbors that would have taken up arms against them!!! And, just so you get a full understanding of how the laws went, if the king decreed that you be put to death, you couldn't fight back. That would be against the law and you would be put to death for that too.

My first thought was - RUN!!!! Remember, we are talking about 4.7 million square miles of land mass for the army to cover in its attack. And since the Jews had a good amount of time to prepare, I thought, why not just high-tail it out of there. Head for Jerusalem, right? They would be safe there, right? Remember when Darius conquered the Babylonians he allowed the Jews to return safely to Jerusalem. So it would only seem logical to me that the families that lived in the surrounding cities would just go there. But, if you look closely at the map of the empire during this time, you will see that Jerusalem sits in the western portion of the empire towards the Mediterranean Sea. To go there would have just made them an easier target.

Something else that caught my eye was in 4:12 and 15. Did you notice anything? When Hathach returns to Mordecai with Esther's message he is not alone. He takes someone(s) with him. The plural "they or them" is used in these verses. That caught my attention and made me wonder. And you all know what happens when I start to wonder about something... yep, I start to do some more wandering. Why would Hathach feel the necessity to take someone with him to converse with Mordecai?

Do you remember ever playing telephone tag as a child? You know. You tell someone something and they tell it to someone else and down the line of kids the message travels until at the very end of the line, the last child tells him what he heard. It is an amazing adventure isn't it. The beginning of the story is most times far different than what the story ends up to be. Why, you ask? Because humans have a way of adding or taking away from a story the parts that either interest them or excite them. It's called embellishment. In our excitement we tend to add a little bit here and there to make the story that much better. Oh, we don't really mean to exaggerate per se, but alas, it happens. This is one of those instances where retelling exactly what was told to him must be just that... EXACT!! Hathach cannot afford to bring the Queen anything but the exact words of Mordecai and maybe that is why he chooses to take someone with him. There is safety in numbers, folks.

In verses 10-11, Esther reminds Mordecai that she cannot just go and have a cup of coffee with the king and chat with him about this situation. The Persian law forbade it. They did not share an ordinary husband/wife relationship at all. She only went to see him IF he called for her, and that was usually for one thing and one thing only. Entertainment. They did not get together each evening to go over the events of their day and just sit and visit by the fireside. To approach the throne of the king without his expressed permission resulted in death. To anyone. Even the Queen.

You can read as much agony as you can into Esther's response. But in short form it was "No". Plain and simple. She would not go into the king and speak to him about this matter. She would not risk being put to death. A part of me wonders if Esther really didn't get the seriousness of the entire matter. To say no to her cousin seemed almost heartless to me. But then I had to ask myself....
"Haven't you ever put your own needs first Ms. Downer?????" "Haven't you convinced yourself that you wouldn't be able to change things so why rock the boat and try????" Haven't I, like Esther, found myself safe and secure in my own world and afraid to reach out and do the right thing because, well, my world might not be so comfortable anymore?

But dear old Mordecai, ever the rationalist shakes her out of her imaginary world of comfort and says "So you really think that this doesn't affect you my dear cousin? Do you really think that at the end of the day, when this is all said and done, the all powerful and mighty King Ahasuerus won't be told that YOU are also a Jew? Can you really trust all of those servants to keep your little secret???" Now mind you, I am aware that scripture doesn't say it quite exactly the way I have said it. Remember... we talked about telephone tag earlier. No matter how the words are given, she must understand fully, that she, the Queen of Persia, will also be put to death when the year's time is up.

What will Esther do? How will she respond to this bit of truth that she must now face? Once a decree, always a decree. Once a Jew.....

Chapter 38

Throughout our study and within the pages of the commentaries I have read, most scholars ask the same question about this great book of Esther, "Why no mention of God?" Not once will you find His name in these many verses. Not once will you read the words of Mordecai and Esther as they call out to Him to save His people. Why? Because they didn't verbally *say* anything about doing that. It is like He has almost been forgotten... or has He?

When Mordecai sends the famous words to Esther, "Yet who knows if you have come to the kingdom for such a time as this" (4:14), we need to remember something about her. She was brought to this kingdom by her cousin after her parents had died. She was not born here. She had previously lived outside of the citadel with Jewish parents. It reminds me of Ruth in a way. When Ruth married into the Jewish family she learned about the culture and beliefs of Naomi and Elimelech. Esther possibly knew who the Lord God was, but like so many others, had made the choice to live outside of His will. And once again, I find myself asking this question, "Lord, have I too known your will and desire for me, but made a choice to live apart from it?"

And here is why I ask this question. In her response to Mordecai she gives him direct instructions for not only for the two of them but for all the Jews that he could gather to him. She tells him to fast. This would not have been an instruction that she would have given him IF she didn't know that it was of the Jewish culture to fast in times of distress. The Persians certainly didn't do it, nor would the Babylonians, at least not to the same God. It was a Jewish cultural ritual to fast to the Lord, the same as wearing sackcloth and ashes. Only the Jews would have known the significance of her command to Mordecai.

And yet Esther includes her own maids in the fasting too. By including them she has just let everyone within her own safety net know that she too was a Jew. To say at this point that she is now vulnerable would be an understatement. But isn't that when the Lord works in us the best? When we cast aside our own desires and put Him first.

If you close your eyes you can almost picture Esther taking a deep breath, tossing her head back, placing her hands on her hips and proudly and yet humbly declaring that she would at that very moment put her entire life and future in the Lord's hands. Because when she says the words "and if I perish, I perish," she has a full and complete understanding that her reward for doing the right thing will be blessed by the Lord, and that that blessing could very well be after her life is over. In other words, she realized the heavenly reward was far better than the earthy comforts of the palace.

And that, my friends, is where I see the working sovereign Lord once again. Her soul told her what to do. Her spirit became one with the Lord and she responded. Oh, you may tell me that the word "pray" is not actually written here, and I will wholeheartedly agree with you. But the concept of the fast, from the Jewish culture was so that the people who fasted could focus entirely on the problem at hand. In the discomfort of the hunger pangs was the constant reminder of the problem. And since the problem here was with God's people, I can't help but feel that at some point in the fasting and contemplating that the Lord Himself would again come to her mind and also to Mordecai's mind.

When I have wandered far from the loving path and guidance of the Lord, I will readily admit, like Esther and Mordecai, I wasn't thinking of the Lord at all. As a matter of fact, when I think about it, it would be near impossible to stray like that AND think of Him. Don't you agree? But, when the gravity of my own situation, my own bad choices has hit me head on, it is then, that I look to the heavens and seek His face. Maybe in their own way, fasting was their way to reconnect with the Almighty Lord God. Heaven knows they all needed Him right about now.

So Mordecai turns for home and Esther contemplates her decision and her next move. She has three long days to fast and prepare. Will that be enough time? For me, three days is *just* right!!

Chapter 39

"And so I will go to the king, which is against the law; and if I perish, I perish!" 4:16.

Before we move on into chapter 5, I wanted to contemplate this verse for just a minute or two. I have a couple of ideas that the Lord showed me about myself (go figure, huh?) and I wanted to share them with you and see if you feel the same way.

I must tell you that I enjoy our studying together because now I actually read the verses and think about them instead of only reading them. Each time I sit down here to write, I ask the Lord again to touch my heart with the message He needs me to understand and at the same time bless my writing so that I may convey what He shows me to you. In other words, to get "me" out of the way. I try not to put my own spin on anything, but I do share things that come to me in response to what I have read and studied. This last passage was no different.

In reading this section several times now, I have come to the conclusion that it could be interpreted in a couple of different ways. Depending how you perceive the situation would define your reaction and then action. Let me explain what the Lord revealed to me about... well, me.

When I really started thinking about Esther's response "If I perish, I perish!" I thought to myself, now there is a girl who is 100% in agreement to the plan. She is totally on board with what needs to be done. She is excited about the decision that was made and will now proceed forward. Or is she???? Could it have been that she is just resolved to what she has been asked to do and is just doing it... well... because that is the only course or action to take? Hmmm.

Now this thought made me think about myself and the times that I have had to make a decision to do the "right" thing. Oh, I may have made it, but I was kicking and screaming the whole time!!! Have you ever done that???? We know what needs to be done. As a matter of fact, we know what *should* be done, but there is this part of us that so very much wants to do it our own way in our own time that we get in the way. It's like saying, "Fine !! Whatever!!" We become almost bitter in our spirit because even though the decision is the right one for everyone involved, it means that we somehow have to do something that we didn't really want to have to do. Like teaching Bible study on Sunday morning. Or helping out in the nursery to give someone else a break. Or working full time to help support our family. How joyfully do I do those things when asked????

The Lord showed me in this passage that I needed to be "heart smart." Have an attitude of gratitude. Maybe I need an adjustment on my entrustment. I am His, bought with a price so high that I couldn't pay it if He asked me to. When there comes an opportunity to do for HIM through what I do for others, I need to see the blessing and not the inconvenience. Ouch, ouch ouch!!!

And I love Mordecai's response and challenge to her when he says, "Look here, *sista* girl. Do you really think that you will be safe from this tragedy? Do you really think that no one within the walls of your palace will point their fingers of persecution against you????" She needed a reality check and he gave her one. Not so pleasant to hear but he spoke the truth to her. She might find safety for a while in her secluded palace, but the decree would eventually find its way to her too. It was the nudge that she needed to turn her heart to the way that it should go.

Sometimes I need a nudge too. Every now and again, I find that a nudge to do the right thing, from the right person, is just what I need. I may not like it when they are nudging me and I may still go kicking and screaming sometimes, but my prayer is that it happens less and less. May I be more "heart smart" and less of an upstart.

Soon Esther's three days of preparation will be over.

Chapter 40

Chapter 5 is where the story of Esther gets busy!! A lot happens within these next few chapters. Things that will not only change the destiny of a nation, but will change the individuals involved as well. Each may try to go his own way, but the Lord God has other plans for them.

It has now been three days since Esther spoke with Mordecai about the decree to kill all of the Jews within the Persian Empire. She instructs Mordecai to gather the Jews in the city for fasting and she and her maids will do the same. And now, the meeting with the king is the next thing on her schedule.

Verse 1 sets the tone for the remainder of our story. Esther is no longer the shy and quiet Jewish girl who just happens to be beautiful and catches the king's eye. No, here we see her for who she has become, a mature woman of stature who is ready, willing, and able to take on this challenge and meet it head on. The Queen of Persia.

When Esther enters the inner court of the king, she is fully prepared for his response. She has come to terms with her duty to her fellow Jews and has come with a plan in mind. But first, she must somehow gain an audience with the king. How better to do that than to stand within his line of vision and look like, well... a vision.

Dressed in her royal robes she awaits the opportunity for him to notice her. She has dressed the part for this royal meeting. Dressing in her royal robes signifies the importance of the meeting and the confidence by which she enters the court. She knows that if the mood is not right, he can strike her down immediately. I read that in Persepolis, another one of the capital cities used by this kingdom, archeologists uncovered a carving with an image of the king sitting on his throne with the golden scepter and right beside him was a man with an axe ready to behead anyone who didn't get the king's approval for a visit.

There were only a handful of people who could enter the kings courts to speak with him and Esther is NOT on that list. Instant death awaits those that the king doesn't want to see. The servant behind him, the one with the axe, is a reminder of what could possibly happen to her for this offense. Plus, she is a woman. She has absolutely NO rights at all. This is beyond a major deal, friends. This is life changing or life ending for her.

When the king glances toward the end of the hallway, he can see Esther off in the distance. She has not entered his "space" but she is close enough to warrant his attention. Funny that none of the guards that stood watch called out to him that there was an intruder. Why? Because she was the Queen and she came dressed for the occasion!! That's preparation, folks.

Have you ever had a meeting or a job interview??? Of course you have. You didn't go dressed in your shorts, t-shirt and tennis shoes did you? No!!! You put on clothing that would put you in the best light for the interviewer to see. I mean, come on now, I would hardly set off on my day to go and see someone of importance with curlers in my hair and no makeup!! My hair all willy-nilly and stickin' up in places it shouldn't. Puh-leeze!! Esther uses one of the tools that she has to her advantage, her royal robes. She knows full well what they signify within the kingdom, and is hoping that the king will know also.

And then she stands, patiently waiting for him to take notice of her. She doesn't go waltzing in to him. She waits. Quietly. Patiently. Respectfully. When you want someone to take notice of you and let you speak, do you run in and interrupt them or do you wait in silence for them to request to hear what you have to say? This is a good lesson for all of us. Esther might have had an emergency on her mind, but she sought the aid of the king quietly. In doing so, he noticed her and wanted to hear what she had to say. Patience is sometimes our best offense when we need a good defense.

And how will the mighty King of Persian respond to her?

Chapter 41

I have asked myself why Esther would prepare a banquet for the king, and I think I have an answer. Pride. If there is one thing that we have learned about King Ahasuerus, it is that he is a prideful man. He liked to show off and to be shown a good time. We learned that fact back in the first chapter. She clearly knows how to get his attention. A banquet in "*his*" honor. My, my, my, what a smart idea.

Although the queen herself wouldn't have been in the palace kitchen with her Betty Crocker apron on and flour all over her face, she would have had some input as to what the servants made. The menu would have been designed by her and orchestrated in such a way as to be pleasing to the king, her husband. Remember the old saying "The way to a man's heart is through his stomach?" Well, Esther does know that the rich and wonderful food and drink is indeed something that her husband enjoys so she uses it as a tool in her plan to speak with him.

In verse 3 the king graciously says "What do you wish Queen Esther? What is your request? It shall be given to you- up to half the kingdom." Quite flattering when you think about it. She hadn't even invited him to the banquet yet and he is offering her half of his kingdom. Now most scholars would say that he didn't really mean it in that way. That he was just extending to her a warm welcome. But I ask you this. When you have family stop by do you offer them half of what you own simply because you are pleased to see them???? I doubt it. Although, he may not have expected her to take him up on the offer what if she had???? That could have changed everything. She could have said "I would like to see a certain group of people moved out of the kingdom as they are due to be annihilated next year. How's about you sign a decree stating that they cannot be killed as long as they stay within that half of the kingdom?" Problem solved.

Ah, but Esther had something other than just saving her people on her mind I think. She intended to bring an evil man before the king. Haman. Notice in verse 4 she requests that the banquet include Haman as well. Doesn't that strike you as odd? It made me wonder why the king wouldn't have questioned her motives as to why she wanted his Prime Minister there. But, as we have learned from past experience, King Ahasuerus doesn't pay close attention to these things. He was probably just thinking of the honor of having this banquet and didn't give her request to include Haman much thought.

Now, it is not like the king didn't eat very well every night, folks. He had a plethora of delicacies that could have been brought to him any day or time. Breakfast, lunch, or dinner would have been a vast array of choices. But a banquet? Well, this signifies that the food and the atmosphere would not have been an everyday eating ritual. And we all know that the king likes a good party!!

"And at the banquet of wine......" (vs. 6). Wait a minute here. Who said anything about a banquet of wine???? Countless times and countless numbers of people have held meetings and made decisions while attending the "banquet of wine." It seems, perhaps Esther is using a tool that the king loves, in this case wine, and using it to her advantage. While he and Haman toast to their wonderful greatness, she is quietly off in the corner awaiting just the right time to speak to him. When the chance arises to speak to him (vs. 7) she politely replies that she would like to do this again tomorrow and then she will let the king know her request.

Can't you just almost see King Ahasuerus and Haman kicking back on satin cushions, filling their goblets over and over again with fine wine, and having servants keep their platters of food well stocked? They wanted for nothing. All was right in their world. Or was it?

Chapter 42

In Esther 5:9 we see that the banquet is over and Haman is joyfully leaving the palace merrily on his way home. The scripture even says he had a glad heart. In other words, he was feeling pretty good. And who wouldn't be? He was the second in command of the most powerful empire in the world and he was loved and respected by all of his friends and associates. Whoops. Did I say *all*????

As Haman is leaving the palace he can't help but notice that Mordecai is there at the gate and once again Mordecai does not show him the respect that he feels that he deserves. In the very same verse that claims that his heart was joyful and glad, we now read that he is filled with indignation. What a contrast of feelings. It must have felt like having a bucket full of ice water tossed in his face. I can almost picture him coming out of the palace whistling a happy little tune and then stopping in his tracks and raising an eyebrow in disgust as he peers over at Mordecai. Oh, the thoughts that he must have been thinking.

But notice he held his tongue. For whatever reason, he says nothing and just continues to go home. Have you ever found yourself in a position like this where you just held your tongue? Oh, you had words you wanted to say, but you didn't. The tongue can be our worst enemy at times. When our feelings are hurt or we are angry, we often times say things that we wish we could take back, but can't. Silence is indeed golden at times like that, wouldn't you agree?

But then he shakes himself off and makes his way home and calls for his family and friends to come over and hear all about his day!!

There is nothing better to help cure a bruised ego than a bit of bragging. And quite a bit of bragging it is. He lets them all know in no uncertain terms just how important he really is. His great wealth. His multitude of children. His promotion and advancement in ranking within the kingdom. It's as though they didn't even *know* him!! But wait a minute here. These are his family and friends remember. They already know all of these things about him so why is he telling them again? Can anyone say, PRIDE???

His pride is speaking for him. He is boasting of who he is because his pride tells him that he deserves more than what he is getting. The thorn in his side is Mordecai. He even tells them how the Queen herself has invited only him to join the king at another special banquet. And yet in the same breath (vs. 13) he admits that it is all for nothing because that Jew, Mordecai is still sitting at the kings gate. All of his blessings of wealth, power, family and authority in the kingdom are overshadowed by one man, Mordecai, the Jew.

And then Haman's friends and his wife gather around him and come up with a plan to take care of the situation. Fire Mordecai and hire someone else to work in that area? NOT!! Nope. They decide that the only way to cure the situation is to "build a gallows 50 cubits high and in the morning suggest to the king that Mordecai be hanged on it." Right about here I asked myself if the whole lot of these folks had continued on with the wine banquet when Haman got home. A 50 cubit gallows is approximately 8 stories high!!! Yes, that's right, I said EIGHT stories!!! And they're just going to toss that together overnight? Do you think anyone might notice????

Why is it that our most irrational thinking will most often times produce the most irrational behavior? It is as though we can't stop ourselves from spiraling out of control in order to try and gain control. In this case, one man's control over another. It sounds like old Haman really has his work "cut" out for himself. It doesn't sound like anyone is going to get a peaceful night's sleep in this kingdom does it? Someone is going to be quite busy chopping and building all night long.

Chapter 43

"That night the king could not sleep," begins chapter 7. Well who could've slept in the kingdom with all of the noise that Haman and his construction crew were making. Oh I know, the palace would have been far away and very much sheltered from any of the noise from Haman's building team but isn't it odd that on this very same night the king is tossing and turning? Coincidence? I think more of a God-instance.

Have you ever had a sleepless night? One where you tossed and turned and couldn't get comfortable no matter how you tried? You were too hot so you threw off the covers. Then your feet got cold. Your pillow (that you used to love) became a brick under your head. Any number of things can keep us from a restful sleep. Worry. Stress. Rich food. Unanswered questions. The king had gone to bed with a mystery that hadn't been solved remember? Queen Esther never told him why she wanted to have another banquet for Haman and him. Maybe these thoughts kept him awake. Or maybe it was the rich food and too much wine??? Or maybe Someone else had a plan for him that night.

When the king couldn't sleep he called one of his servants in to read to him. Not so unusual at all. In fact, he could have requested any number of servants to come and entertain him if that is what he wanted. He had a harem full of beautiful women at his beck and call. He had musicians that could have soothed him with soft melodies to ease him to sleep. A masseuse to rub the kinks out of his tired shoulders. The list is endless. Yet, out of all of the choices he had, he chooses to be read to. And he doesn't pick just any old book either. He has the records of the chronicles of the kingdom read to him. What???

Here is a definition of the term chronicle, "a usually continuous and detailed historical account of events arranged in order of time without analysis or interpretation." Can anyone say "yawning"? Maybe that is why the king called for this particular book to be read to him. It would be boring and hence put him back to sleep. Can't you just almost see the mighty King Ahasuerus propped up in his bed, a bounty of fluffy pillows surrounding him, with a nice warm glass of milk balanced carefully in his hand, nodding off to sleep from the reading of the daily happenings at the city gate? And the poor servant. Sitting there trying to stay awake and reading by candle light, facts and figures from the daily business dealings. Boring, boring, boring! Enough to put someone, well, back to sleep.

The chronicles were the actual historical happenings within the city of Shushan. The heartbeat of the kingdom so to speak. The comings and goings of the peoples. The buying and selling of properties, land and materials. The legal matters of the day that were recorded at the city gate. Marriages. Births. All kinds of information pertaining to the daily life recorded for the king and for the future of the empire. Persian history books in the making.

But something in the reading catches the king's attention. You see, the servant just happens to read to him the part about the assassination plot involving Bigthan and Teresh from five years ago!! Do you remember them? Just after Esther had been made queen and Mordecai was working at the city gate, he overheard the two eunuchs plotting to kill the king so he told Esther and she told the king (2:21-23). If you notice in 2:23 it says "it was written in the book of chronicles in the presence of the king." This is the exact same book that the servant is now reading to the king on this sleepless night!! I ask again... Coincidence or God-instance?

King Ahasuerus's immediate response is "what honor or dignity has been bestowed on Mordecai for this?" (6:3). You see, the Persian monarchs were firm believers in rewarding those that were loyal to them. Why? Because loyal subjects could be trusted to protect them from the disloyal inhabitants of the kingdom. People just like Bigthan and Teresh lived in the city and roamed the streets awaiting an opportunity to do away with a monarch they didn't like or agree with. We still have countries and people like that today. Rewarding those who were faithful and loyal to the monarch was not only the right thing to do, but a smart thing as well.

As the king ponders his predicament, an unexpected guest arrives in his court. Who could it be so early in the morning? Who would dare to come to the king's bedchambers unannounced at such at a time as this?

Chapter 44

"What honor or dignity has been bestowed on Mordecai for this?" asks the king. And after a long sleepless night, his weary servant responds "Nothing has been done for him." (vs. 3)

At this point both the king and the servant have realized that a man of honor, a man who showed loyalty to the king and to the mighty Persian Empire has been totally ignored and overlooked and it burdens the king greatly. He must rectify the situation. He must somehow make it right and bring honor where honor is deserved. But how? He needs to consult with someone who can advise him on this most delicate situation. And just then he hears a noise and asks, "Who is in the court?"

Now remember, it is still very early and the king is probably not expecting visitors. But when he hears that it is Haman come a-callin', well, he tells the servant, post haste, to "Let him come in." I must admit that I really don't know too much about the bedclothes that kings wore back then and I didn't really want to take up precious time with research on it so allow me one small moment of... well... my own vivid imagination.

As Haman enters the private inner chamber of the king, he is greeted by the rich smell of aromatic Persian coffee simmering away in a silver carafe just beckoning him over to share a cup and a chat. He looks up and sees the king, *his* king, with his hair all tussled from sleep, probably very long in fact, since they weren't known for haircuts back then, and maybe pulled back into a ponytail, but loose... with strands all this way and that, some even sticking up here and there. Because of the early hour and because the king wasn't aware that Haman was coming over for this visit, his is still in his jammies. Now I know, right about now, even *you* are smiling at this picture. The mighty King of Persia caught off guard in his 'feety' jammies!! Hey, it could happen.

As Haman is escorted into the room, the king immediately launches into his inquiry about honoring a man for his good deed to the kingdom. And Haman, immediately thinks that the king MUST be talking, well, about *him*!!! After all, he thinks, who could be more deserving of the kings honor? I can just picture him tap, tap, tapping his pointy little finger to his cheek as he pretends to give the matter much deep and sincere thought. He might have even paced around the room a few times in a dramatic show of concern that the king handle this matter with the utmost care.

And so, ever the good event planner, he lays an idea before the king that is sure to please. Look closely at the things that Haman is requesting for the honoree to receive in verses 8-9. Go ahead....read them a couple of times and see if you see the significance here. The items that Haman is so coyly suggesting be used to honor himself (and remember, he really thinks the king is talking about honoring him) are fit for a king because they ARE for a king!!! If Haman would have thought for one minute that the king was paying homage to someone other than himself I venture to say that he never would have suggested this kind of a show. To be paraded around the town for all to see in the kings robe, riding on the kings horse, with the kings crest on its head, well, that's pretty "kingly" wouldn't you say? It is almost like a coronation for a new king. As a matter of fact, I don't have to read between too many of the lines to see that Haman may have very well seen himself in this exact position. As the new King of Persia. Something to think about...

But wait. It is time for Haman to pull his head out of the clouds and get back to the business at hand. You see, the king *loves* his idea and wants him to go and proceed with the plans right away. Remember how Haman had suggested that one of the king's most noble princes would do the honor of escorting this fine honoree through town? Well that just won't do at all. No, no, no. This man, this highly-regarded, most honorable man deserves the very best escort, the king tells Haman. "And that escort must be none other than YOU!!"

It is probably right about now that Haman is concentrating on picking the invisible lint off of his jacket so as to hide his utter surprise and dismay from the king. If he is the one to be the escort, then it is obviously NOT him that the king is finding the need to honor. And then his proverbially bubble burst as the king says "Hurry and do all that you have suggested for Mordecai the Jew. Leave nothing undone that you have spoken." (vs. 10)

You can almost feel the air being sucked right out of Haman's lungs. What is he supposed to say? How is he supposed to respond? Hours before he and his merry band of carpenters had built a 50 cubit tall gallows to hang Mordecai on. His problems were to be solved. And now, he was required to parade that very same problem around the entire town proclaiming the king's delight in him.

And so, bowing from the waist to show respect to his king, Haman slowly begins to exit the room. But I got to thinking. Didn't he originally come early to talk to the king? Remember? Haman had a request of his own for the king. What if, and this is a big what if on my part, but what if the king remembers and just as Haman is making his way back out of the room he says "Oh Haman, you came early to speak to me. What is it that you have need of my loyal friend?" And under his breath in almost a whisper you hear Haman mutter the words, "Never mind......."

Chapter 45

"Afterward Mordecai went back to the king's gate. But Haman hurried to his house, mourning and with his head covered." (vs. 12)

One man shows humbleness by the act and the other is humbled because of it. Pretty good contrast.

Once the parade and celebration are finished, Mordecai returns to finish his work day and Haman rushes home with his tail tucked between his legs. Now mind you, no one in the town has been made aware of the reason that Haman went for that early morning visit with the king. Unless of course that someone noticed the 50 cubit tall gallows off in the distance and perhaps asked someone about it???? Gossip travels pretty fast, even in faraway places like Shushan.

But there is one very important thing that everyone in the city was well aware of. Remember that there was a decree from the king to kill all of the Jews. And that very decree had been designed by none other than Haman, written by Haman and sent out by Haman. Do you think that maybe some of the townsfolk, Jews and non-Jews, were scratching their heads at the irony of Haman parading Mordecai around the town in this celebration?

I cannot stress enough to you about the value that the other citizens would see in the wearing of the king's robes. These robes would have been a treasure within themselves. Mordecai would have most likely been given the robe to keep because the king would never have worn it again since it had been worn by another person. Talk about a family heirloom to pass down. But what is far more important here, is what it signified to the people of the citadel. Mordecai was being called out by the King of Persia, and publicly recognized for his faithful service, loyalty and trust. His coworkers, friends, family and neighbors would have understood this huge honor and at the same time wondered how it was that in just a few short months this same man was going to be executed along with all of the rest of the Jews in the empire!! Talk about being perplexed.

But here is something else that has perplexed me. When the king realized that Mordecai had never been honored for his act of bravery and loyalty, he immediately sought a way to correct the problem. Even if it meant having a bit of egg on his face. After all, it has been five years since the incident happened. But the king knew it was the right thing to do, so he set aside his own ego and went about correcting the wrong. But here is the perplexing part. Did you notice in verse 10 the king says "Mordecai the Jew?" Doesn't it seem to you that he would have questioned the prudence of honoring a Jew since not so long ago he had sent out a decree to have them all, including Mordecai, killed? He doesn't even take that into consideration here. Could it be that maybe he *still* is not aware of just who this group of people is that Haman has deemed as disloyal to the kingdom????

And as Haman arrives home, do you think he finds his loving wife and friends and family waiting to greet him with words of encouragement. NOT!! After he tells them the horror and embarrassment he has endured, it is his wife that shakes her head and proclaims "If Mordecai, before whom you have begun to fall is of Jewish descent, you will not prevail against him but will surely fall before him." (vs. 13) What does she mean IF he is of Jewish descent? Is she asking? Like she doesn't know???

Look back at 5:14 again. It is Haman's wife, Zeresh and his friends and advisors who convinced him to build the gallows to hang Mordecai on. Yet now her words almost put the blame of the entire situation back onto Haman, as though he had withheld important information in the decision making process. It's as though she is saying, "Wow, if I would've know THAT, I would never have said...".

She and his friends have shifted the responsibility of the bad outcome to Haman and left him holding the bag.

I am in no way feeling sorry for Haman nor am I trying to portray him as a victim here. But, in all of my readings each day, I always ask the Lord to show me the things that He needs me to see and learn about myself and to see for others as well, if possible. This section struck me in a way that I didn't expect at all. It is about cause and effect. Wanting what you want when you want it and stepping on anyone's toes to get it, and then standing back and crying the blues when your world starts to crumble around you. So I need to pose a few pointed questions to myself and I will share them with you.

Do I walk around with a Haman attitude during the day demanding that my co-workers, neighbors, family and friends respect me because, well, I am ME? Do I walk by the city gate just seething under my breath because I don't get the pay I think I deserve, the respect I know I should get or the accolades that surely should be mine? When a fellow citizen of my town gets his day in the sun do I show up for his parade waving a flag and shouting his name joyfully or do I stand off in the back of the crowd just waiting to go back to my own little cubicle with a painted smile on my face that could crack and dissolve into a million pieces at any moment? Carrying around a grudge has brought Haman to where he is now. A place that has brought him humiliation and, in due time, if nothing stops it, will bring others to annihilation.

"While they were still talking with him, the king's eunuch came, and hastened to bring Haman to the banquet which Esther had prepared." (vs. 8)

Oh, that's right. How could I forget? Haman still has another banquet to go to. Lucky him. He gets to spend some quality time with the King and Queen of Persia all by himself. Won't that make him feel just all kind of special? Maybe this will bring him just the honor and respect he has been looking for or maybe...

Chapter 46

As we begin chapter 7, King Ahasuerus and Haman have once again joined Queen Esther for a private banquet. Most likely, this banquet is taking place in her section of the palace in her own private living quarters and garden area. They begin as they did the day before with wine, and again the king asks her, "What is your petition, Queen Esther?"

"If I have found favor in your sight, O king, and if it pleases the king, let my life be given me at my petition, and my people at my request. For we have been sold, my people and I to be destroyed, to be killed and to be annihilated. Had we been sold as male and female slaves, I would have held my tongue, although the enemy could never compensate for the king's loss." (vs. 3-4)

The king has given Esther permission to ask for anything. Anything that she wants. He even says again, "up to half of the kingdom." Now mind you, he doesn't exactly mean "half of the kingdom" here. That is just an expression. But it is a sincere gesture on his part to listen to her and to fulfill her request. It shows that he genuinely cares about her.

Esther's true character, one of humbleness and meekness, one of pure gentleness and integrity shines through in her opening statement to the king when she says, "If I have found favor in your sight." Remember, she is the Queen of Persia. Her attitude is not one of haughty greatness for the title she holds. She is not expecting him to listen to her request nor respond to her request simply because of the title she carries. Unlike some *other* person in the room sitting at the same table, I might add. She has come to him with a request and will present it to him honestly and will expect him to handle it in an honest fashion, if given the opportunity. Unlike some *other* person sitting at the same table, I might add again.

There are a couple of things in her statement that we need to look at. First, she made the king aware that the people were sold. Someone is getting the money for them. People were bought and traded all of the time. That was nothing new. As a matter of fact, as hard as it is for me to write about it, we still have slave markets and slave trading that goes on today in our societies and even our own country. Men, women and even children are bought and sold and used for any number of illicit activities. Don't even get me started on the subject of human trafficking. It is just heartbreaking!!

But to sell them for the sole purpose of killing them???? What was she talking about? And who was she talking about? And wait a minute... Did she say HER people????? Can you just imagine for a moment the look on Haman's face when King Ahasuerus yells across the table, "Who is he, and where is he, who would dare to presume in his heart to do such a thing?"

And suddenly we see the contrast of Haman's completely pale white face and the bright red wine he has no doubt just spilled staining the lovely hand woven white linen table cloth (that might just surely be a family heirloom) as he begins to sputter and cough as Esther turns and points at him and says "The adversary and enemy is the wicked Haman." (vs. 6)

In just a split second and with just a few words from Queen Esther, the reputation and honor of Haman has been destroyed before the eyes of the king. There is absolutely nothing that he can say or do at this point. Haman is speechless. You see, he had no idea that decree he so coyly crafted to do away with all of the Jews would include the Queen of Persia!

In a fit of rage, the king leaps from his perch on the settee at the banquet table and storms outside where he paces in the gardens. I can almost envision him grabbing hold of the table and literally tossing it and its contents across the room on his way out. This is not a king that holds his temper well as we have seen in past circumstances. And now, not only has he heard his wife, the queen, say some disparaging things about his Prime Minister, but he has found out that she is a Jew and that she is slated to be killed along with a group of people that in reality he didn't even have a problem with!! Now who's perplexed???

Haman makes two very critical errors in judgment in these next verses and seals his own fate. He approaches the Queen to plead for his life after King Ahasuerus goes out into the garden. In Persian culture he should have never *ever* been in the room alone with a woman that belonged to the king. And the Queen belonged to the King. Period. He should have high-tailed it out of there and waited for the king to come back in. But instead, Haman approached Esther and actually falls at her feet begging for his life and when the king comes back into the room, well he sees it and becomes even further enraged and says, "Will he also assault the Queen while I am in the house?" Wow! No one puts their hands on the property of the king. NO ONE!!

And just like that the king's attendants cover Haman's head and prepare to lead him away to his death. Harbonah, one of the king's eunuchs, says, "Look! The gallows, fifty cubits high, which Haman made for Mordecai, who spoke good on the king's behalf, is standing at the house of Haman" Then the king said "Hang him on it." (vs. 9) Pretty amazing that Harbonah just happened to make mention of that now, isn't it? Or is it? Coincidence? I think God-instance.

The gallows that Haman had built to hang Mordecai on and display his body for the entire town to see was now used for him. In Persian culture, the gallows was most times heavy "stakes" where the body was actually impaled, not hung from a rope like we think in western culture. It is a gruesome and horrifying public display. With the body being placed that high in the air (8 stories), you can only imagine what the sun and the birds would do to it.

As Haman is led away, the king is left with his queen and his thoughts. There are still many questions to ask, and just as many answers to give. A part of me wonders if it might be time for our royal couple to sit down and have a heart-to-heart chat. For such a time as this.

Chapter 47

A lot has happened in the last few verses of chapter 7. King Ahasuerus was faced with the fact that his trusted and loyal servant, Prime Minister Haman was not so trusted and loyal after all. The chapter ends with Haman being hanged on the gallows that he had built for Mordecai and, "then the king's wrath subsided." (vs. 10) The KJV uses the word *pacified* which is the translation of the Hebrew work *shakak*, which is used in Genesis 8:1 describing the receding waters of the Flood.

Have you ever been so angry that you reached the boiling point? Something happens or someone says something to you, and before you know it, BANG! You are so mad you can hardly see straight, let alone think straight. Words are spoken, voices are raised and feelings are hurt. Sometimes the damage is so great it takes years to repair, if it is even ever repairable. James 1:19 reminds us to, "let every man be swift to hear, slow to speak, slow to wrath;" Too many times I forget to "count to 10," or "take a big deep breath" before I say what is on my mind. How about you?

When King Ahasuerus stormed out of the banquet, he was full of rage. His ego had just taken a major blow. His wife had just informed him of some very important pieces of information regarding his empire that he wasn't even aware of. The entire Jewish population within the empire was slated to be executed and oh, by the way, she was a Jew. When he demands to know who it is that has done this horrible thing she turns and says matter-of-factly, "The adversary and enemy is the wicked Haman!"

At first when I studied this, I thought that she was referring to Haman in those terms for *her* benefit, but you know what, I don't think so anymore. I think she was very smart and knew that the king would recognize those terms in regards to his kingdom. In other words, she was saying that Haman was an adversary and an enemy of HIS kingdom!!! Now that will get his attention for sure.

The Jewish population was approximately 15 million people at this time. They were hard working, tax paying citizens of the Persian kingdom. Esther's point was well taken by the king. If they would have been sold for profit, that would have been one thing, but to be killed? The only one who benefited was Haman since he would have claimed the plunder. The king had no idea of who was even being executed. So the words she used were chosen very wisely and the king fully understood them.

"On that day King Ahasuerus gave Queen Esther the house of Haman, the enemy of the Jews." 8:1. I am such a romantic, that a part of me, a big part of me, I must admit, wanted this mighty king to take just a moment and go over and put his arms around his wife and say the words that every person in the world longs to hear when they have been wronged... "I am sorry." I know, I know, I am a dreamer. Maybe by presenting her with this vast amount of property and wealth, it was his way of saying it without really having to... well... you know... say it.

In Persian culture the property of a traitor would have been confiscated by the king to add to his own wealth. In this case, for whatever reason, King Ahasuerus gave all of Haman's estate to his wife. But what could she possibly do with it? After all, she is the Queen of Persia. She already has a palace for goodness sake. She wants for nothing. What does she need another large home and property for? Oh, but wait. She has another family member that might be able to use it. Perhaps you remember him? His name is Mordecai.

"And Mordecai came before the king, for Esther had told how he was related to her."8:1 Think back, many years ago, it was Esther that had told the king that Mordecai had warned her of the plan of Bigthan and Teresh to assassinate him. This is the same Mordecai that just a few hours ago, Haman had paraded through the streets on a royal crested horse, wearing the royal robe of the king, being honored by the king for his loyalty. And now, this same man is found to be the king's cousin by way of marriage!!!

In Esther 8:2, the king immediately gives Mordecai his signet ring. Do you remember who had it previously? That's right. Haman. So, as Haman was being led out of the banquet hall with his head covered, someone had the wherewithal to get the ring for the king and give it back to him. That ring was the absolute power for the kingdom and for the king to be without it would have been devastating. Some commentators suggest that Ahasuerus gave it to Mordecai too quickly. Not that Mordecai was not a good choice or anything like that, but just that it once again showed how Ahasuerus tended to act in the spur of the moment. Much like when Haman got his job in the first place.

As with all good decisions, they must be thought out carefully and not made under duress. As we have seen throughout this book, King Ahasuerus is not one to think things through. He has been impulsive in his decision making and it has proven to be costly. His decision to allow Haman to write a decree to annihilate the Jews cannot be revoked. It is set in stone. The date is set. The Persian law cannot be changed. There is no amount of money and no amount of power that can change the decree of death to these innocent people.

But maybe, just maybe, there is a way. Could it be that Mordecai and Esther now live in the Persian palace by coincidence? Or could it be a God-instance?

For such a time as this, my friends, for such a time as this.

Chapter 48

As we continue on in our study in chapter 8, Queen Esther is again in conversation with King Ahasuerus. Look closely at verses 3-4. She is at his feet begging for his mercy for the Jews. Then he "held out the golden scepter toward Esther." In other words, he once again allows her to have an audience with him. In my reading and studying, I had somehow let chapters 7 and 8 kind of blend together with no passing of time. But the writer has made it clear to me that there must have been time in between because now Mordecai is there and Esther has sought permission to speak again.

I must admit this timeline made me wonder about the conversation that the king and queen might have shared. If there is one thing that I have learned after several years of marriage is that silence is *not* always golden. There are times when you just really need to talk things out. Ephesians 4:26 tells us, "Be angry, and do not sin, do not let the sun go down on your wrath." I don't know about you, but for me, going to bed with an angry, bitter heart produces tossing and turning and a sleepless night. My mind is busy, busy, BUSY, talking, talking, TALKING to myself about all the things (not nice, either) I should have said to prove my point etcetera, etcetera, etcetera... The alarm goes off in the morning and I look and feel like something the cat dragged in off of the streets!! That in itself, is a reason NOT to go to bed mad!!

In his anger and frustration at the situation, the king could have easily dismissed Esther to her quarters. He could have just as easily called in the same group of princes and advisors that had so readily given such rapid fire advice regarding Vashti and sent Esther packing. He could have done any number of things in a fit of rage. But do you know what he did? He extended grace where he didn't have to. He showed mercy to someone who needed it.

We don't really know much about Esther personally until this moment. By that I mean within the previous verses of the book, there is not much written about her to define her character. But here, in these verses you can *feel* her heart. She is pleading to the king for those who cannot plead for themselves. She is willing to give up her life to redeem the lives of others. Her example here is much the same as when our Lord Jesus offers His redemptive love for us, my friends.

As I pointed out before, Persian law is unchangeable. But, where there is the will of the Lord, there is also the way of the Lord. King Ahasuerus instructs Queen Esther and Prime Minister Mordecai to come together as a team and put on their thinking caps and write a new decree that would reverse the old one!! They have his blessing and his signet ring, as well as his full staff of scribes to assist them in the task. Now it is time to get busy!

Have you ever heard the sayings, "strike while the iron is hot" or "get while the getting is good?" These phrases mean to get your act together and get 'er done!! Many times when situations that need our action arise we have a tendency to maybe spend a bit more time on the planning/decision making than is needed. We form committees and have meetings, which are good, but sometimes, not always, sometimes... well, the meetings seem to take on a life of their own and become a personality contest or a battle of will. We can lose focus on the issue and only concentrate on getting our own way. Discussion and planning are good as long as they are kept in perspective.

Time is not on Esther and Mordecai's side here, folks. Two months have already passed since Haman sent out the first decree. There is not much time to get the new decree written and translated into the many languages of the empire. It is a daunting task, to say the least. But once again, I am reminded that although I might not see the name of God written within these verses His power and sovereignty are displayed. "For I know the thoughts that I have toward you, says the Lord, thoughts of peace and not of evil, to give you a future and a hope." Jeremiah 29:11. Sweet words of blessing that I have cherished many a time.

In verse 9, the very first group of people that Mordecai addresses are the Jews. You might ask yourself why. Well, the answer is simple. It is because the first decree that went out was *about* them. This one is *for* them. They didn't even get a copy of the first decree. You see, the Jews were now being given permission to defend themselves. What??? Oh you didn't know they couldn't defend themselves???? Well, they couldn't. According to the Persian law, if the king ordered that you be killed, you would be breaking the law if you defended yourself. So you would then be killed for defending yourself!!! The Jews were totally and undeniably between a rock and a hard place. They never would have had a chance. But now, because of the words of the new decree, the ability to defend themselves has been granted. There is now singing in the streets of Shushan.

I can almost picture Queen Esther standing in the window of the palace looking out over the kingdom as the couriers ride swiftly through the gates. Taking in the view, Esther watched in quiet and humble peace. Prime Minister Mordecai, dressed in his magnificent royal robes, in the colors of the Persian Empire, a golden crown sitting on his head, was met by the joyful cries of his fellow countrymen. The very ones who were set to die. The very ones Esther chose to redeem.

Where is God in all of this you ask?

Right where He needs to be!

Chapter 49

This next section of the story of Esther had me baffled for awhile. I really had a hard time with Esther's attitude and her response to the slaughter and destruction around her. I saw an Esther I had not seen before. One that I hardly recognized.

On the thirteen day of the twelfth month of Adar, those that came against the Jews were met with fierce opposition. Have any of you asked yourselves why this battle even took place? I know that I have. I kept mulling it over in my mind and I just kept wondering why these so-called "neighbors" took up their weapons against the Jews in the first place. They had all lived side by side for many years so why did they follow through with the original decree to slaughter all of the Jews?

GREED.

Remember, Haman had promised *big* money to those who would pick up their weapons and annihilate the Jews. This wasn't a "war" that the Persians were in. This was not about the Persian army marching down the streets and taking the Jews captive. This was based solely on a hatred of one race for another, started by one very powerful man at the time, Haman, and it was fueled by his promise of monetary gain. Knowing that the Jews could not defend themselves against the onslaught made it easy money. Military men and non-military men alike were promised a certain amount of money for their participation in the complete destruction of the Jews. And as an added bonus, anything they gathered as spoil belonged to them as well.

But when Mordecai came into power as the Prime Minister and wrote the new decree, that changed everything. The Jews were now granted permission to protect themselves fully from anyone that threatened them with harm. This did not give the Jews permission to go on the offensive but they could defend themselves to the point of killing their attackers. The decree also gave the Jews permission to plunder the possessions of those they killed because Mordecai was doing an exact reversal of the original degree. The instructions were very clear in the wording. Very clear. But they took nothing of the plunder because God's law instructed them not to. It too, was very clear.

We see in Esther 9:3 that the people in Shushan "feared" Mordecai. The Hebrew word here is "*pachad*" meaning actual fear. Not as in reverence, awe, respect kind of fear. But a shake in your boots kind fear. Why? How is it that this man has gone from a quiet, well-respected "man at the gate," to one who is now feared by the "officials of the provinces, the satraps, the governors, and all of those doing the kings work?" I am burdened in my spirit that the author has chosen to use the word "fear" here to describe how others react to him and to his leadership. Surely, I tell myself, it must simply be a form of translation issue. Mordecai couldn't have become a man that others feared, could he?? As the Prime Minister of the great Persian Empire, is he so full of the thirst for power that he has become someone that we no longer recognize from the previous chapters? I think the reason for the fear is simply the fact of the power that he wielded.

"Thus the Jews defeated all their enemies with the stroke of the sword, with slaughter and destruction, and did what they pleased with those that hated them." (vs. 5) Wow! This does not paint a very pretty picture at all. Total chaos prevailed in the streets throughout the entire empire. It was a bloodbath. The Jews and their allies massacred 500 men in the citadel in Shushan alone. Plus the ten sons of Haman were killed. The tables had turned on those that wanted to destroy the Jews.

Back in the safety and quiet of the palace, the news is brought to the king and queen. The king turns and asks the queen what else she desires. This is the fourth time that King Ahasuerus has asked

Queen Esther to share her heart's desire with him. I conclude by these gestures that they did have a relationship. He cared for her. He wanted to please her and make her happy. He wanted to correct a wrong that he had done. In either his laziness or ignorance, he had set the wheels in motion on this train wreck and maybe he felt compelled to try and fix it.

Her response absolutely flabbergasted me. "Let the Jews who are in Shushan do again tomorrow according to today's decree, and let Haman's ten sons be hanged on the gallows." (vs.13) Can I get a "whoa Nelly" from somebody out there, please????

How in the world does this request possibly make any sense at all? Now I admit, I am not a rocket scientist here folks, but my goodness, even I can figure out that she seems to be overstepping what was intended by the decree that she and Mordecai wrote. Oh, I am not talking about the ten sons of Haman on the gallows. I get that. Even though they were already dead, the display of their dead bodies was done as well, just that... a display.

But clearly the other part of her request needs a tad bit more looking into.

Chapter 50

As we continue on in the final verses of chapter 9 and 10, Queen Esther has taken on a new personality. Gone is the quiet meekness of the beautiful young Jewish girl Mordecai first brought to the palace. What seems to have emerged is a bold, outspoken leader, a woman who possesses the ability to get what she wants when she wants it.

As the news of the activities" in the citadel is brought to the palace, the king and queen discuss the outcome. After telling Esther how many men have been killed, the king then asks her if there is anything else she wants done. I just can't help myself, but I just have to ask... who's in charge here???? Her or him? And please don't miss another very important little tidbit that the author didn't include here either. On the other occasions when Esther was talking with the king, the author made a point to write that the king extended the golden scepter to her and *allowed* her to speak. This time there is no mention of that at all. Each time, it is noted that the king allows her to speak to him. It is as though the writer wants us to understand the importance of the role change.

Queen Esther's role in the kingdom has changed. I think see that from these verses and the way that they are written. She has taken on a new responsibility of leadership and respect. It is apparent that the king values her judgment and opinion in this matter. The situation is dealing with *her* people, the Jews. And the outcome, the future peace and prosperity of the Persian kingdom, needs to be addressed, handled, and dealt with. Because, like it or not, the reality is, that now, within the royalty of the Persian government, the Queen and the Prime Minister are Jews. The political power has shifted. The Jews within the Persian Empire now have a voice and they are going to be heard!!

When King Ahasuerus asks Queen Esther what else she thinks needs to be accomplished she replies "If it pleases the king, let it be granted to the Jews who are in Shushan to do again tomorrow according to today's decree, and let Haman's ten son's be hanged on the gallows." As I mentioned before, I had a really hard time with this verse and Queen Esther's new found attitude, until I really gave it some thought and some study. She seemed so hard and so cold, so different from the young girl who had first come to the palace. But you know what? She was different. She has grown up. She has accepted the responsibility of not only being the Queen of Persia, but guiding the destiny of her own people.

When she replies to the king to "do again tomorrow according to today's decree," I had to give that some thought. Does she know something that I don't know? Remember, the decree that she and Mordecai wrote is one of defensive measure not offensive. Obviously she knows enough about human nature to know that the Jews might just need that second day to protect themselves and to send out a message, loud and clear, to anyone inside the citadel limits. This was indeed a very political move on her part and a very smart one at that. You see, the Jews now had come into power politically with her as queen and Mordecai as the Prime Minister.

The ten sons of Haman are even named individually within the verses of Esther 9:7-9. It is as though the author wants us to hear loud and clear that justice has been served. They are all hung on the gallows in the citadel for all to see, just as their father had been. This puts an end to the Amalekite's line, just as the Lord had commanded so many years earlier. The difference here is that the plunder was not touched by the Jews. In these verses we are told three times that nothing of the plunder was taken, unlike Saul, who took the things he shouldn't have and then dared to try and justify his sin before the Lord (read 1 Samuel 15).

The very next day another 500 hundred enemies of the Jews were killed bringing the grand total to 75,810 throughout the entire empire of Persia. It's a big number when you think about it isn't it? It makes my heart sad for all the hatred felt that brought the people of this nation to this point. Because, as I said before, it wasn't a war between nations, it was a war between neighbors.

There was much rejoicing in the citadel and in the surrounding cities. And they had much to rejoice about didn't they? The Lord God Almighty, had placed two very ordinary people, Esther and Mordecai in a position to do what needed to be done if they were obedient. And they were. Through their obedience, the Jewish people thrive. One man's evil plot was thwarted by the faithfulness of God and His people.

Mordecai sent word to all of his countrymen that they should indeed celebrate this wonderful victory. God should be honored and praised each year and the occasion remembered. Instructions were written and a decree from King Ahasuerus was sent out to all of the surrounding cities that everyone should celebrate on the fourteenth and fifteenth days of the month of Adar each year to remember the great victory of God's people.

To this very day each year our Jewish friends still celebrate Purim. It is a time to get together, have a large feast, give gifts and party, party, party!!! It is a time when they read every word of the book of Esther and remember a young Jewish girl that stood tall and proud and when the time came to do the right thing she said,

"I will. And if I perish, I perish."

If asked to do the same for our Lord and Savior would we too say those same words? He did for us what we could not do for ourselves. Romans 5:8 tells us, "But God demonstrates His love toward us, in that while we were still sinners Christ died for us." His gift of salvation is so perfect and so complete there is nothing that we can add to it. We just need to accept it. I pray that you have done that.

Are you willing to be obedient for such a time as this?

I hope and pray that you are!!!

God has great things for you to do.

People to encourage.

Lives to change.

May God bless you!

Nansii

www.ingramcontent.com/pod-product-compliance
Lightning Source LLC
LaVergne TN
LVHW051520080426

835509LV00017B/2124